CARLA BLYTH HUGHES

PRENTICE HALL REGENTS, Englewood Cliffs, New Jersey 07632

Hughes, Carla Blyth
Top the TOEFL Test: Ten days to a Higher Score / Carla Blyth Hughes
p. cm.
ISBN 0-13-064973-2
1. Test of English as a Foreign Language—Study guides.
2. English language—Textbooks for foreign speakers. 3. English language—Examinations—Study guides. I. Title.
PE1128.H76 1994
428' .0076—dc20
94-7682
CIP

Aquisition Editor: *Nancy Baxer*
Director of Production and Manufacturing: *David Riccardi*
Electronic/production and interior design: *Paula D. Williams*
Editorial Production/Design Manager: *Dominick Mosco*
Cover Design Coordinator: *Merle Krumper*
Production Coordinator: *Ray Keating*

Cover Illustration: *Ruta Kysilewskyj*

Prentice–Hall, Inc.
A Paramount Communication Company
Englewood Cliffs, New Jersey 07632

Printed in the United States of America
10 9 8 7 6 5 4 3 2 1

ISBN 0-13-064973-2

Printed on Recycled Paper

Prentice Hall International (UK) Limited, *London*
Prentice Hall of Australia Pty. Limited, *Sydney*
Prentice Hall Canada, Inc., *Toronto*
Prentice Hall Hispanoamericana, S.A., *Mexico*
Prentice Hall of India Private Limited, *New Delhi*
Prentice Hall of Japan, Inc., *Tokyo*
Simon & Schuster Asia Pte. Ltd, *Singapore*
Editora Prentice Hall do Brasil, Ltda., *Rio de Janeiro*

To Mum, Dad Carmen, and Cliff

With love always

INTRODUCTION

Before you start on the Ten–Day TOEFL Plan take a few minutes to read this introduction; - it will tell you what this book can and can't do for you. No book can improve your English in only ten days, so if that's what you expect from this plan you are bound to be disappointed.

So what can you reasonably expect from following this plan? Although it may be impossible to improve your English in ten days, you can expect substantial improvement in your TOEFL taking abilities. How? By becoming familiar with the exam format and learning what to expect; by absorbing pointers that will help you achieve the highest possible score with what you already know; by learning the key vocabulary items that make memorizing long word lists unnecessary. Are you ready? Then turn the page and begin the plan. Remember, the key to improving your score is BELIEVING you can do it. This book will show you how!

CONTENTS

GET READY

Take a few minutes to plan how you will use this book.

- You will need at least 90 minutes each day (with a short break).

- Try to study at the same time each day.

- Choose a convenient time when you know you are at your best. Don't plan to set your alarm early if you **know** that won't work. Another bad time is right after a big meal, like lunch or dinner. Pick your time slot carefully, and then stick to it.

- Find a place that is reasonably quiet and make sure you have paper and pencil handy.

- You will also need a cassette player on Days 1, 2, 3, and 10.

Ready?– It's time to work!

OVERVIEW: KNOW THE TOEFL FORMAT

Any test, including the TOEFL, becomes much less of a worry once you know what to expect. It's important that you become familiar with the TOEFL format as soon as possible. Each day *TOP THE TOEFL® TEST* will enable you to work through a particular section of the exam.

The TOEFL TEST consists of three sections ALL of which contain multiple choice answers.

Section 1. LISTENING COMPREHENSION:
(Parts A, B, and C)
50 questions in 40 minutes

Section 2. STRUCTURE AND WRITTEN EXPRESSION:
(Parts A and B)
40 questions in 25 minutes

Section 3. VOCABULARY AND READING COMPREHENSION:
(Parts A and B)
60 questions in 45 minutes

NOTE: If you are taking the TOEFL on specific dates you will also be required to take the Test of Written English (TWE) ®. The TWE is administered in addition to the TOEFL but scored separately. It is NOT optional. Check the Testing Calendar at the front of your TOEFL® Bulletin of Information to see if the TWE® is scheduled.

If you find that you will be taking the TWE, make sure you read through Appendix 1 at the end of this book. You probably need an extra day or two for this.

Now look at each section of the TOEFL in more detail:

SECTION 1: LISTENING COMPREHENSION

This section lasts 40 minutes

It has a total of 50 questions

It is divided into THREE parts (A, B, and C) all of which require listening to recorded speakers.

Part A: STATEMENTS

You hear various sentences on the tape. You must choose the answer which is most similar.

Part B: SHORT CONVERSATIONS

You listen to several short conversations between two people. Then you choose the answer to the single spoken question that follows each conversation.

Part C: MINI-TALKS AND LONGER CONVERSATIONS

You listen to mini-talks or longer conversations. These will be followed by several spoken questions and will require more specific information. Listen carefully. Important information is often repeated during each conversation or mini-talk.

It's important to remember that all recorded material will be heard only ONCE! You are not allowed to take notes.

SECTION 2: STRUCTURE AND WRITTEN EXPRESSION

This section lasts 25 minutes.

It has a total of 40 questions.

It is divided into TWO parts.

Part A: STRUCTURE

You must choose the word or phrase that will best complete a sentence.

Part B: WRITTEN EXPRESSION

You must identify which part of a sentence is INCORRECT.

SECTION 3: VOCABULARY AND READING COMPREHENSION

This section lasts 45 minutes.

It has a total of 60 questions.

It is divided into TWO parts.

Part A: VOCABULARY

You must choose the word or phrase which could replace the underlined part of a sentence.

Part B: READING COMPREHENSION

You will read several passages and choose the correct answers to the questions that follow.

Don't worry if all this seems confusing. By the end of the *TEN DAY PLAN* you will be fully familiar with each section and every part of the test. Remember, once you know what to expect you will begin to feel confident about taking the TOEFL Test.

DAY 1

Part 1
Introduction to the Exam Format

When you register for the TOEFL you will receive a copy of the *TOEFL® Bulletin of Information* published by *Educational Testing Service*. This is a valuable booklet, so keep it handy. In addition to explaining how to complete the registration form, the bulletin contains important information on procedures and regulations, plus a short selection of practice questions.

Remember, the TOEFL test is divided into three sections:

1. Listening Comprehension (40 minutes)

2. Structure and Written Expression (25 minutes)

3. Vocabulary and Reading Comprehension (45 minutes)

Today you will start working on the first, the Listening Comprehension section, which lasts forty minutes. This section is designed to test your knowledge of English as it is spoken in North America. There are three parts.

Part A

You will listen to short statements or sentences on the tape. Each will be followed by a 12–second pause. During this time you will read four sentence choices in your test book and choose the one that is closest in meaning to the sentence you heard. In other words, find the sentence that says the same thing in a different way. Then fill in the corresponding oval on your answer sheet.

Your Strategy—What You Need to Know

This may seem to be the easiest part of the test, but you still need complete concentration. You will hear the sentence on the tape only once. The short pause is long enough for you to make your choice but there's no time to waste! Remember that you are not allowed to mark or write in your test book. You need to be alert.

Work through the examples below. As you hear each sentence try to break it down into simple facts.

REMEMBER: Press the PAUSE button after each sentence so you can work through the explanation at your own speed.

START THE TAPE NOW

You will hear: (Listen then pause)

Example I

This means:

Two people finished the painting job in four hours.

One person would have taken eight hours.

THIS IS WHAT YOU WILL READ:

(A) It was too difficult a job for one person to do.
(B) It would have taken three people four hours to do the painting job.
(C) It would have taken me eight hours to do the painting job on my own.
(D) Only a very fast painter could finish the job in time.

Pay particular attention whenever you hear a number mentioned, because that is often a clue to the answer. In this case you would need to remember four hours for two people. Also listen for key phrases like "half the time" or "twice the time" as these tell you whether to divide or multiply the number.

Now look at the sentence choices again on page 2. Look at the explanations b elow:

(A) This is an opinion and has nothing to do with the sentence you heard. Ignore it.
(B) There's no mention that it would take three people as long as two people to do the job. Ignore it.
(C) Here the numbers fit: one person–eight hours (4 x 2). This looks like the correct answer, but read (D) just in case.
(D) This is just another opinion. Ignore it.

The correct answer is (C). On your answer sheet, fill in the oval for (C) next to the right question number.

The next example is similar.

Example II

You will hear: (Pause)

This means:

The game started at 6 o'clock.

They arrived at 6:15.

THIS IS WHAT YOU WILL READ:

(A) They got there at five forty-five.
(B) They got there at six.
(C) They got there at a quarter after six.
(D) They got there at six-thirty.

Pay special attention to the two numbers mentioned on the tape—six o'clock and fifteen minutes. The key word here is *late,* which makes it six fifteen. What's another way of saying 6:15? The correct answer must be choice (C) "a quarter after six."

Ⓐ Ⓑ ● Ⓓ

Example III

You will hear: (Pause)

This means:

Jim's father is my brother.

I am Jim's uncle.

Jim is my nephew.

THIS IS WHAT YOU WILL READ:

(A) Jim is my brother-in-law.
(B) Jim is my nephew.
(C) Jim is my cousin.
(D) Jim is my uncle.

Quickly decide how Jim is related to you. Your brother's son is your nephew. So the correct answer is choice (B)

Ⓐ ● Ⓒ Ⓓ

Example IV

You will hear: (Pause)

This actually means:

Annie was on vacation when her mother got sick.

Annie went home as soon as she heard her mother was sick.

THIS IS WHAT YOU WILL READ:

(A) Annie could not go on vacation because her mother was sick.
(B) Annie was able to enjoy part of her vacation.
(C) Annie delayed her vacation until her mother was better.
(D) Annie went home after her vacation.

Pay special attention to the key phrase cut short. It means that Annie's vacation was shorter than expected because her mother became ill. Now look at the sentence choices again on page 4. Look at the explanations below:

(A) Ignore this. You know that Annie was already on vacation when her mother became ill
(B) True. Annie was on vacation before she went home, but first check out the remaining choices.
(C) No. *Cut short* does not mean delayed. Also you do not know whether her mother recovered.
(D) No. Annie was unable to complete her vacation as planned.

The sentence choice closest in meaning is choice (B).

(A) ● (C) (D)

Example V

You will hear: (Pause)

This means:

Jake and his father are doctors.

Jake's grandfather is also a doctor.

THIS IS WHAT YOU WILL READ:

(A) Jake wants to be a doctor.
(B) Both Jake's parents are doctors.
(C) Jake decided not to be a doctor.
(D) Jake's grandfather is a doctor.

The sentence you heard tells you that Jake, his father, and his grandfather are all doctors (Don't let phrases like *his father's father* confuse you.)

It's easy to find the correct sentence choice.

(A) Jake is already a doctor.
(B) Jake's mother was not mentioned.
(C) You were told the three chose the same profession.
(D) Correct!

Ⓐ Ⓑ Ⓒ ●

NOW YOU TRY

Try the short exercises that follow. Listen to the sentences on the tape, then try to pick out the correct sentence choices as quickly as possible. (You will find the answers at the end of the exercise.)

This time do not press PAUSE after each sentence. Try to complete the question during the 12 second pause.

1. (A) Students will have to wait until spring for the test results.
   (B) The exam results were mailed to the students.
   (C) The test results will be ready early in the fall.
   (D) Students may take the exams again in October.

Ⓐ Ⓑ Ⓒ Ⓓ

2. (A) Last year's motorcycle would have cost $2,400.
   (B) Last year's motorcycle would have cost $2,600.
   (C) Last year's motorcycle would have cost $3,000.
   (D) Last year's motorcycle would have cost $3,400.

Ⓐ Ⓑ Ⓒ Ⓓ

3. (A) Rose's mother lost about 3 pounds.
   (B) Rose's mother lost 10 pounds.
   (C) Rose's mother lost 14 pounds.
   (D) Rose's mother lost 8 pounds.

Ⓐ Ⓑ Ⓒ Ⓓ

4. (A) I failed the test.
   (B) I needed more time to finish the test.
   (C) I did well on the test because I had studied hard.
   (D) Despite my studying, I found the test difficult.

Ⓐ Ⓑ Ⓒ Ⓓ

5. (A) A new computer would cost $750.
   (B) A new computer would cost $3,000.
   (C) A new computer would cost $3,500.
   (D) A new computer would cost $4,500.

Ⓐ Ⓑ Ⓒ Ⓓ

Turn off the tape. Check your answers below.

ANSWERS

1. (C) The results come out in October.
   October = the fall.

2. (B) This year's new motorcycle cost $3,000.
   Last year's new motorcycle cost $2,600.

3. (C) Rose lost 7 pounds on the diet.
   Rose's mother lost 14 pounds.

4. (D) I studied hard for the test.
   I thought the test was difficult.

5. (B) A second-hand computer costs $1,500.
   A new computer costs $3,000.

If you found the exercises difficult, try again with the tape. Read the tapescript which is printed at the back of the book, <u>only</u> if you continue to have errors.

DAY 1

Part 2
Vocabulary Warm–Up

Your Strategy— Improving your Vocabulary

Part 2 of the Daily Plan will not follow the TOEFL test format. Instead it will provide a workout for the skills you will need to complete the sections of the exam that will follow during the next nine days.

Several TOEFL prep books include long lists of common words used in the TOEFL that are very useful for long-term study. Although it's impossible to try to memorize a large number of new words in just ten days, there are certain things you can do.

CONTEXT: If you don't know the meaning of a word, first try to use the other words in the sentence to help you figure out what the word means. In other words, the sentence may provide the clue. If not, check the surrounding sentences and make a good guess. This means you should use clues to infer the meaning. For example, find what the word *beverages* means in the context below.

> Several beverages were offered at the reception. I chose coffee, but there were also tea, soft drinks, and even wine.

Looking at the sentence in which the word *beverages* occurs is not very helpful. You learn only that *beverages* are served at a reception. The sentence that follows, however, tells that *beverages* means drinks in the general sense of the word.

Remember that context can be very important in helping you find the meaning of an unfamiliar word.

WORD PARTS: Another way to determine the meaning of an unfamiliar word is to analyze the different parts that make up the word. Many words can be split up into three parts: base words, prefixes and suffixes.

Base words are short words that form the core or center of longer words. Look at the list below and see if you can pick out the base word in each.

carefree   uncaring   careless   careful

The base word is *care*. The meaning of each of these words has been extended by adding a syllable (a *prefix*) before the base word or by adding a syllable (a *suffix*) at the end of the base word. Sometimes both a prefix and a suffix are added to the same base word.

If you know the meaning of the base word and the prefix or suffix used, you can to figure out what the new word means. Therefore, learning the meaning of a few useful prefixes and suffixes can quickly increase your vocabulary.

The prefixes listed in Table 1.1 mean *not*. These change a base word into the opposite of what it originally meant. Remember that all the prefixes in the table mean *not, the opposite of,* or *lack of.*

Table 1.1

Prefix	Example	Meaning of prefix + base word
dis–	discomfort disadvantage	lack of comfort or no comfort lack of advantage or no advantage
non–	nonverbal nonviolent	not verbal not violent
un–	untried unsuspected	not tried not suspected

The prefix *in* – also has the same meaning of *not* (*the opposite of*) or *lack of*. This prefix changes slightly however, depending on the first letter of the base word it is joined onto (see Table 1.2).

Table 1.2

Prefix	Example	Meaning of prefix + base word
in–	inexpensive inadequate	not expensive not adequate
il– (before l)	illegal illogical	not legal not logical
im– (before b) (before m) (before p)	imbalance immoral impatient	lack of balance not moral not patient
ir– (before r)	irregular	not regular

You do not need to memorize the variations of the prefix *in-*; just make sure you can recognize them.

PRACTICE TIME

Using the prefixes you learned above, figure out the meanings of the following words.

1. incurable
   (A) able to be cured
   (B) unable to care
   (C) unable to be cured
   (D) lacking in care

   Ⓐ Ⓑ Ⓒ Ⓓ

2. nonbreakable
   (A) not broken
   (B) not breakable
   (C) damaged
   (D) replaceable

   Ⓐ Ⓑ Ⓒ Ⓓ

3. disgrace
   (A) elegance
   (B) lacking gratitude
   (C) without honor
   (D) full of grace

   Ⓐ Ⓑ Ⓒ Ⓓ

4. irresponsible
   (A) without a response
   (B) not responsible
   (C) not responsive
   (D) involved in responsibility

   Ⓐ Ⓑ Ⓒ Ⓓ

5. unlimited
   (A) without limit
   (B) very limited
   (C) able to be limited
   (D) setting a limit

   Ⓐ Ⓑ Ⓒ Ⓓ

Check you answers below.

1 (C) 2 (B) 3 (C) 4 (B) 5 (A)

BE CAREFUL

Remember that not *every* word contains a prefix, even though it may appear to. Always check the base word before you try to determine the meaning of an unfamiliar word.

First remove the prefix to see if the remaining base is really a word. If the base makes sense, you're dealing with a prefix. If it doesn't, there is no prefix.

For example, *immobile* has *mobile* as its base word. The prefix *im-* changes the meaning to "not mobile." But removing *im–* from *imagine* would leave *agine* as its base word. This does not make sense, so *im–* is not a prefix here.

DAY 2

Part 1
Listening Comprehension – (continued)

Today you will continue working on the Listening Comprehension section of the TOEFL. Yesterday you practiced Part A. Today you will be practicing Part B.

Part B

You will hear two people having short conversations on the tape. These will be followed by a third person who will ask a question about each conversation. You will then read four possible answers in your test booklet and choose the best answer to the question.

Your Strategy—What You Need To Know

Remember that you will hear the conversation and the question only once, so you need to pay full attention. The conversation is usually easy to follow, but you need to listen for details, such as where the conversation takes place (in a library? at a travel agency?); the speaker's occupation (doctor? cook? teacher?); and the relationship between the speakers (husband–wife? teacher–student? doctor–patient? friend–friend?)

Listen to the speaker's tone of voice. The way a person says something can often give you a good idea of what is being said. Which words are emphasized by the speaker? Is he or she angry, relaxed, surprised, or annoyed? Remember—you're listening with a purpose.

Below are examples of the types of questions you will find in Part B of the TOEFL test, Listening Comprehension section.

Press the PAUSE button after each conversation to allow you time to answer the question at your own speed. The standard 12–second TOEFL pause will not be used for these examples.

START THE TAPE NOW

You will hear: (Pause)

Example I

You should have understood that:

Barbara works at the Admissions Office.

She is sick with the flu.

She will be back at work on Monday.

THIS IS WHAT YOU WILL READ:

(A) She quit her job.
(B) She was from the Admissions Office.
(C) She was out of town.
(D) She was sick.

The correct answer is choice (D).

(A) (B) (C) ●

Example II

You will hear: (Pause)

You should have understood that:

The woman asks the man to help her the next day.

She wants to clean out the garage.

He will be free after lunch.

THIS IS WHAT YOU WILL READ:

(A) Show her the way to the nearest garage.
(B) Have lunch in the garage.
(C) Help her clean out the garage.
(D Park her car in the garage.

The correct answer must be choice (C).

(A) (B) ● (D)

NOW YOU TRY

You will probably find Part B is easier than Part A, because a spoken conversation between two people is often easier to follow than a single sentence. Remember to listen for these details: Who? What? Where? When? Why?

Try the short exercises that follow. Listen to the conversations and questions on the tape, then look at the corresponding answers below. (You will find the answers at the end of the exercise.)

This time do not press PAUSE after each sentence. Try to complete the question in the standard 12–second pause on the tape.

START THE TAPE NOW

1. (A) She changed her mind after she bought it.
   (B) She doesn't think it's pretty.
   (C) She got it as a gift but doesn't like it.
   (D) She doesn't like the color.

   (A) (B) (C) (D)

2. (A) Five o'clock.
   (B) Six o'clock.
   (C) Six-thirty.
   (D) Seven o'clock.

   (A) (B) (C) (D)

3. (A) He's gone out of business.
   (B) He was too busy to come today.
   (C) He was out all morning.
   (D) His phone wasn't working.

   (A) (B) (C) (D)

4. (A) To enter the country.
   (B) To get a driver's license.
   (C) In order to cash some checks.
   (D) In order to claim travel expenses.

   (A) (B) (C) (D)

5. (A) In a department store.
   (B) In a restaurant.
   (C) In a travel agency.
   (D) In a drug store.

   (A) (B) (C) (D)

6. (A) They will visit the husband's parents.
   (B) They will stay home.
   (C) They will have lunch at a restaurant.
   (D) They will visit the wife's parents.

Ⓐ Ⓑ Ⓒ Ⓓ

7. (A) To Paris.
   (B) On a cruise.
   (C) On a ski trip.
   (D) To Dallas.

Ⓐ Ⓑ Ⓒ Ⓓ

8. (A) Sell her old car.
   (B) Order a new car.
   (C) Change her plans.
   (D) Go on vacation.

Ⓐ Ⓑ Ⓒ Ⓓ

9. (A) Stay for supper.
   (B) Eat any more food.
   (C) Refuse more vegetables.
   (D) Pass the meat loaf.

Ⓐ Ⓑ Ⓒ Ⓓ

10. (A) A flexible salary.
    (B) A secretary.
    (C) A job.
    (D) A phone number.

Ⓐ Ⓑ Ⓒ Ⓓ

Turn off the tape. Check your answers below, then take a short break before going on to Part 2.

ANSWERS:

1 (C)	3 (D)	5 (D)	7 (A)	9 (B)
2 (B)	4 (C)	6 (D)	8 (D)	10 (C)

NOTE: If you had difficulties, go through the exercises again with the tape. If you still have problems after listening to the tape a second time, read the tapescript, which is printed at the back of the book.

DAY 2

Part 2
Vocabulary Warm–Up

Your Strategy—More Useful Prefixes

Yesterday you studied some prefixes that change the meaning of a word to give its opposite. Today you will look at five more common prefixes. Once you are able to recognize these prefixes, you'll be surprised at the number of new words you will understand. Simply take the meaning of the base word and add the prefix meaning (see Table 2.1).

Table 2.1

Prefix	**Meaning**	**Example**	**Meaning of prefix + base**
re–	back/again	**return**	to turn back/
mis–	wrong (ly) bad (ly)	**misbave**	to behave badly
inter–	among/ between	**interplanetary**	between planets
fore–	before/front	**foresee**	to see in advance
pre–	before	**prepaid**	paid in advance

PRACTICE TIME:

Using the above information, see if you can distinguish the meaning of the following words. Match each word in the first column with its prefix + base word meaning in the second.

Notice the words with an asterisk (*). What is different about them? Remember the warning at the end of Day 1 (Part 2).

Prefix re–: back/again

_____	1. reschedule	(a) to run again
_____	2. rerun	(b) no prefix
_____	3. replay	(c) to plan again
_____	4. replant	(d) to play again
_____	5. ready*	(e) to plant again

Prefix mis–: wrong(ly)/bad(ly)

_____	1. misplace	(a) to understand wrongly
_____	2. misunderstand	(b) to spell wrongly
_____	3. miserable*	(c) to lead in the wrong direction
_____	4. misleading	(d) no prefix
_____	5. misspell	(e) to put in the wrong place

Prefix inter–: among/ between

_____	1. international	(a) to switch places
_____	2. interaction	(b) between different races
_____	3. interchange	(c) no prefix
_____	4. intern*	(d) action between people or things
_____	5. interracial	(e) between nations

Prefix fore–: before/front

_____	1. foremost	(a) to predict beforehand
_____	2. forefather	(b) to warn in advance
_____	3. foreign*	(c) no prefix
_____	4. forewarn	(d) most important
_____	5. forecast	(e) ancestor

Prefix pre–:before

_____	1. precaution	(a) no prefix
_____	2. pretend*	(b) before the proper time
_____	3. precook	(c) before written history
_____	4. premature	(d) care taken beforehand
_____	5. prehistoric	(e) to cook beforehand

Check your answers:

re–	**1.** (c)	**2.** (a)	**3.** (d)	**4.** (e)	**5.** (b)
mis–	**1.** (e)	**2.** (b)	**3.** (d)	**4.** (c)	**5.** (a)
inter–	**1.** (e)	**2.** (d)	**3.** (a)	**4.** (c)	**5.** (b)
fore–	**1.** (d)	**2.** (e)	**3.** (c)	**4.** (b)	**5.** (a)
pre–	**1.** (d)	**2.** (a)	**3.** (e)	**4.** (b)	**5.** (c)

Mixed Practice

Before you finish today, see if you can distinguish the meaning of the following words. Note that Day 1's prefixes are also included.

1. misshapen

   (A) without a shape
   (B) shaped beforehand
   (C) badly or wrongly shaped
   (D) shaped again

   Ⓐ Ⓑ Ⓒ Ⓓ

2. prerequisite

   (A) required beforehand
   (B) without requirements
   (C) wrongly required
   (D) required again

   Ⓐ Ⓑ Ⓒ Ⓓ

3. interlinear

   (A) without lines
   (B) between lines
   (C) wrongly lined
   (D) with lines

   Ⓐ Ⓑ Ⓒ Ⓓ

4. foreword

(A) without an introduction

(B) introduction to a book

(C) without words

(D) wrongly worded

A B C D

5. illegitimate

(A) not according to the law

(B) going before the law

(C) among laws

(D) according to the law

A B C D

6. improper

(A) properly

(B) without property

(C) correct

(D) not correct

A B C D

7. misspent

(A) not spent

(B) spent again

(C) spent wrongly

(D) spent beforehand

A B C D

8. presuppose

(A) to assume or suppose wrongly

(B) not to suppose

(C) to suppose again

(D) to suppose in advance

A B C D

9. disorder

(A) lack of order
(B) order badly
(C) order before
(D) order again

(A) (B) (C) (D)

10. prejudice

(A) a judgment made in advance
(B) lacking in judgment
C) judge wrongly
(D) not judged

(A) (B) (C) (D)

Check your answers below.

Answers

1. (C)	6. (D)
2. (A)	7. (C)
3. (B)	8. (D)
4. (B)	9. (A)
5. (A)	10. (A)

DAY 3

Part 1
Listening Comprehension – (continued)

Today you will start work on Part C of the Listening Comprehension section of the TOEFL test.

PART C

You will hear several mini-talks or conversations. You will then be asked questions about what you have heard. Remember, you will only hear the conversations or speaking selections and questions only once!

The conversations in Part C will be more formal and less friendly than those in Part B. Each question will be followed by a 12–second pause. During this time you must read the four answers in your test booklet, and select and mark the best answer to the question. The questions may refer to facts that were stated or were only suggested in the conversation or mini-talks.

This may seem to be the most difficult part of the test. You will hear a long passage full of facts and details, and be expected to understand and remember much of what is said. The whole test will suddenly seem a lot harder. But stay calm. This is not testing your memory—it's testing your listening skills! Here's what you do.

1. **Concentrate on the tape.** Be alert and listen.

2. **Don't waste time.** Make sure you know exactly what you have to do in this part of the Listening Section before the exam so you do not have to listen to the directions. Instead use this time to read the answer choices. Look over the testbook answers to the first three or four questions **before** the actual speaking begins.

   Stop reading as soon as the speaking begins and **listen** carefully. As soon as you have heard the questions look at the answers again. You will now find that you are able to read and make your choice fairly quickly. You will also have time to preread the answers to the next question.

3. **Let the answer choices help you.** As you read the choices the second time, you may notice that three of the four choices have been mentioned. You can then be sure that the remaining choice is the correct answer to the question. The reverse is also true. If only one of the answer choices is mentioned in the talk, you can assume it's the correct answer.

4. **Be ready to guess!** When the tape moves on you should too. If you do not know an answer, **guess**. Always use the same letter when you guess. Before you enter the exam, decide which letter you'll use and then stick to it. In this way you'll save time and be more likely to score points by chance. If you choose a different letter each time you guess, you might guess wrong every time. But if you always use the same letter you are more likely to guess correctly some of the time.

Relax—it's not as difficult as it sounds. Work through the examples below and see how you do.

Remember to press the PAUSE button after each question to allow you time to answer the question at your own speed. The 12–second TOEFL pause will not be used for these examples.

NOTE: This part of the Listening Comprehension section often starts off with a question about the main idea of what you have just heard.

START THE TAPE NOW

Example I

Next you will hear the following mini-talk:

QUESTION 1: (PAUSE)

THESE ARE THE ANSWER CHOICES YOU WILL READ:

(A) Life at the court of Queen Elizabeth I.
(B) The uses of tobacco.
(C) Sir Walter Raleigh.
(D) Tobacco as an industry.

A quick look at the possible answers will narrow your choices down to (B) or (D). Look for key words before you choose an answer. In choice (D) *tobacco* is a key word, but the mini-talk has nothing to do with *industry*. Choice (B) seems more suitable.

(A) (B) (C) (D)

QUESTION 2: (PAUSE)

THESE ARE THE ANSWER CHOICES YOU WILL READ:

(A) The American Indians.
(B) Sir Walter Raleigh.
(C) Christopher Columbus.
(D) Queen Elizabeth I.

Listen carefully. You're not being asked who made tobacco *popular* in Europe, merely *who took it there*. The answer must be choice (C).

Ⓐ Ⓑ ● Ⓓ

QUESTION 3: (PAUSE)

THESE ARE THE ANSWER CHOICES YOU WILL READ:

(A) 1492.
(B) 1500.
(C) 1555.
(D) 1580.

Forget what you've learned in the past about Columbus. The only date mentioned in the passage was 1580, choice (D).

Ⓐ Ⓑ Ⓒ ●

QUESTION 4: (PAUSE)

THESE ARE THE ANSWER CHOICES YOU WILL READ

(A) Queen Elizabeth I.
(B) Sir Walter Raleigh.
(C) Christopher Columbus.
(D) The American Indians.

The only person mentioned as being so popular that other people copied what he did is Sir Walter Raleigh choice (B).

Ⓐ ● Ⓒ Ⓓ

Example II

As you listen try to simplify what you hear:

The heart beats faster when you run. Why?

- Extra carbon dioxide in the blood stream
- Brain causes heart to beat faster
- More blood sent to the muscles

Next you will hear the following:

QUESTION 5: (PAUSE)

THESE ARE THE ANSWER CHOICES YOU WILL READ:

(A) Blood pressure.
(B) Widening of the arteries.
(C) The circulation during exercise.
(D) Keeping in shape.

Look for key words as you read the choices. Ignore choice (A) because the speaker mentioned movement of blood, not blood pressure. Discard choice (B) because the widening of the arteries was not mentioned. (C) seems to be a good choice since the passage was about what happens when you run a race, but first look at (D). The selection was about physical changes when you run, not specifically about keeping in shape. Therefore, (C) is the best choice after all.

(A) (B) ● (D)

QUESTION 6: (PAUSE)

THESE ARE THE ANSWER CHOICES YOU WILL READ:

(A) Oxygen.
(B) Carbon monoxide.
(C) Carbon dioxide.
(D) Blood pressure.

If you've been listening carefully you'll know that carbon dioxide was the only one mentioned in the selection. Therefore (C) is the correct answer.

(A) (B) ● (D)

QUESTION 7: (PAUSE)

THESE ARE THE ANSWER CHOICES YOU WILL READ:

(A) High blood pressure.
(B) The brain sends nerve impulses to the heart.
(C) Dizzy spells.
(D) More blood is sent to the muscles.

Ignore choice (A): no mention is made of blood pressure, nor of dizzy spells, choice (C). That leaves, choice (B), which is the cause of the heart beating faster, not the result. Therefore, the correct answer is choice (D).

(A) (B) (C) ●

Sometimes Part C will include a conversation, as in the following example.

Example III

Next you will hear the following:

QUESTION 8 (PAUSE)

THESE ARE THE ANSWER CHOICES YOU WILL READ:

(A) New York Harbor.
(B) American history.
(C) The Statue of Liberty.
(D) The sights of New York City.

A quick glance at these possible answers will soon narrow down your choices. Disregard choice (A) because New York Harbor is mentioned only briefly. Choice (B) is too general. Choice (D) is incorrect because only one of the sights in New York was mentioned. Therefore the answer is choice (C).

(A) (B) ● (D)

QUESTION 9: (PAUSE)

THESE ARE THE ANSWER CHOICES YOU WILL READ:

(A) 1882
(B) 1884
(C) 1886
(D) 1888

Listen carefully. Only two dates were mentioned: 1884 and 1886. The statue was brought to the United States before it was erected. Therefore (B) is the correct answer.

(A) ● (C) (D)

QUESTION 10: (PAUSE)

(A) To pay for the statue.
(B) To pay to bring the statue to America.
(C) To pay to have the statue cleaned.
(D) To pay for the pedestal.

This question presents no problems. The American people paid for the pedestal or base. The correct answer is choice (D).

(A) (B) (C) ●

NOW YOU TRY

Try the practice exercises that follow. Remember that Part C of the Listening Comprehension is not testing your memory, it's testing your listening skills. Aim at a general understanding of what is said. Try to let the answer choices help when possible.

This time do not turn off the tape until you have completed all ten questions. Try to answer the questions during the 12-second pause given on the tape.

START THE TAPE NOW

1. (A) A scientist.
   (B) A dentist.
   (C) A counselor.
   (D) A health instructor.

   Ⓐ Ⓑ Ⓒ Ⓓ

2. (A) Join a health club.
   (B) Diet if you are overweight.
   (C) Check with your doctor.
   (D) Purchase the right sportswear.

   Ⓐ Ⓑ Ⓒ Ⓓ

3. (A) Jogging for 20 minutes.
   (B) Swimming regularly.
   (C) Alternating walking with running.
   (D) Walking briskly for 45-60 minutes.

   Ⓐ Ⓑ Ⓒ Ⓓ

4. (A) Poor exercise technique.
   (B) Insufficient rest.
   (C) Being overweight.
   (D) Exercising with weights.

   Ⓐ Ⓑ Ⓒ Ⓓ

5. (A) The name of the pastry.
   (B) Where the man learned to cook.
   (C) Where to buy the pastry.
   (D) The recipe for the pastry.

   Ⓐ Ⓑ Ⓒ Ⓓ

6. (A) The Far East.
   (B) The Middle East.
   (C) The US.
   (D) The Midwest.

Ⓐ Ⓑ Ⓒ Ⓓ

7. (A) By placing it in the freezer.
   (B) By using the ready-made variety.
   (C) By covering it with a damp cloth.
   (D) By rolling it very thin.

Ⓐ Ⓑ Ⓒ Ⓓ

8. (A) The San Isidro festival was held there.
   (B) Madrid was chosen as the cultural capital of Europe.
   (C) The Summer Olympics were held in Spain.
   (D Madrid was voted Europe's top tourist center.

Ⓐ Ⓑ Ⓒ Ⓓ

9. (A) March.
   (B) Early spring.
   (C) May.
   (D) Late autumn.

Ⓐ Ⓑ Ⓒ Ⓓ

10. (A) Around the Plaza Mayor.
    (B) Along the main highways.
    (C) On the outskirts of the city.
    (D Close to the San Isidro festivities.

Ⓐ Ⓑ Ⓒ Ⓓ

NOW TURN OFF THE TAPE

Check your answers below, then take a short break before going on to Part 2.

1. (D)	3. (D)	5. (D)	7. (C)	9. (C)
2. (C)	4. (A)	6. (B)	8. (B)	10. (A)

NOTE: Try this section again with the tape if you need to. Read the tapescript only if you still continue to have problems. It is printed at the end of the book.

DAY 3

Part 2
Vocabulary Warm-Up

During the past two days you have seen how new words are formed by adding prefixes to the beginning of base words. Today you will look at suffixes–word parts that change the meaning of a base word by being added to the end of the word. For example, in the word *beautiful*, the suffix is–*ful.*

Adding a suffix sometimes changes the spelling of the base word. In the example above, the *y* at the end of *beauty* changes to *i* before adding *–ful*. Some base words drop the final letter when a suffix is added. For example, style + *–ish* becomes stylish; *love* + *–able* becomes *lovable*. Don't worry about these possible changes, just be aware of them.

The suffixes listed in Table 3.1 below are among the most common. Once you're able to recognize them, you'll be surprised at the number of new words you can guess the meanings of. Begin by looking at these five suffixes which are commonly used to form adjectives.

Table 3.1 Common Suffixes

Suffix	**Meaning**	**Example**	**Meaning of base + suffix**
-ful	full of	**harmful**	full of harm
-ous	full of	**joyous**	full of joy
-less	without	**useless**	without use
-able	capable of being	**lovable**	that can be loved
-ible	having...	**sensible**	having sense

PRACTICE TIME:

Use the information given above to see if you can match the following words with their meanings.

Note: This exercise does not follow the TOEFL test format, but it will improve your vocabulary skills for Section 3 of the exam.

_____	1. cheerful	(a) fond of study
_____	2. breakable	(b) grateful; expressing thanks
_____	3. thunderous	(c) without joy; gloomy
_____	4. cheerless	(d) well-known; celebrated
_____	5. studious	(e) full of envy
_____	6. washable	(f) full of cheer; joyful
_____	7. thankful	(g) easily broken
_____	8. famous	(h) ungrateful; without thanks
_____	9. envious	(i) producing a loud noise like thunder
_____	10. thankless	(j) can be easily washed

Check your answers below:

1 (f)	3 (i)	5 (a)	7 (b)	9 (e)
2 (g)	4 (c)	6 (j)	8 (d)	10 (h)

Suffixes can also be used to create nouns—a person who does a thing or an abstract noun (for example, *amazement* = the state of being amazed). The most useful suffixes are listed in Table 3.2

Table 3.2. Common Suffixes that Create Nouns

Suffix	Meaning	Example	Meaning of base + suffix
–er/–or	person or thing that does	**actor** **computer**	person who acts a machine that computes something
–ist/–ian	person who	**physicist** **guardian**	person who knows physics person who guards
–ment	state or quality of being	**enjoyment**	the act of enjoying
–ness	state or quality of being	**happiness**	the state of being happy

MORE PRACTICE

As you did in the previous exercise, use the suffix information given above to match the following words with their meanings.

_____ 1. admirer (a) the state of being sad

_____ 2. electrician (b) a device that amplifies

_____ 3. encouragement (c) a person who admires

_____ 4. sadness (d) one who survives

_____ 5. director (e) the act of encouraging

_____	6. amplifier	(f)	quality of having a quick mind
_____	7. librarian	(g)	person who works with electricity
_____	8. survivor	(h)	person in charge of a library
_____	9. contentment	(i)	person who directs or rules
_____	10. cleverness	(j)	the state of being content

Check your answers below.

1 (c)	3 (e)	5 (i)	7 (h)	9 (j)
2 (g)	4 (a)	6 (b)	8 (d)	10 (f)

SECTION 1 SUMMARY

Listening Comprehension Section of the TOEFL Test

This section lasts 40 minutes.

It has a total of 50 questions.

It is divided into THREE parts A, B, and C. Each part involves listening to recorded speakers.

PART A: SENTENCES

You hear various sentences on the tape. Choose the answer which restates what you have just heard.

PART B: SHORT CONVERSATIONS

You listen to several short conversations between two people. Then choose the answer to the one spoken question that follows each conversation.

PART C: SHORT SELECTIONS AND CONVERSATIONS

These will be followed by several spoken questions and will require more specific information. Listen carefully since the information is often repeated during the coversation or mini-talk.

Remember that all recorded material will only be heard once!

You may not take notes!

DAY 4

Part 1

What You Can Expect to Find in Section 2 of the TOEFL Test

Structure and Written Expression (total time 25 minutes)

The second section of the TOEFL test is completely different. You must now read formal written English. You will have twenty-five minutes in which to complete 40 questions. There are two parts (A and B) and there are two types of questions. Each type requires a different strategy.

PART A: STRUCTURE (Incomplete Sentences)

You will read a sentence that has a word or phrase missing. You will then choose, from the four choices written below, the word or phrase that best completes the sentence. There is only one correct answer.

Read all the examples that follow and make sure you understand how the correct answer was chosen. Each example is similar to the type of question that may appear on the test.

Example I (Verb tense)

I am still here because I ____________ my train to Washington.

(A) almost missed

(B) almost miss

(C) just will miss

(D) just missed

You need to choose the correct verb tense. The subject of the sentence, (*I*) is still here because of something that happened before now. This means you can ignore choices (B) and (C), which refer to the present and future time, and are incorrect because of *just* and *almost*.

Choices (A) and (D) are both in the past tense. See if the adverb can help. The word *almost* in choice (A) means that the person speaking was able to catch the train although just barely This is incorrect because the speaker is still at the train station. The correct answer must therefore be Choice (D).

THE SENTENCE SHOULD READ:

I am still here because I just missed my train to Washington.

(A) (B) (C) (D)

Example II (Conditional sentence)

Will you give this message to Tony if he ___________?

(A) came
(B) is coming
(C) will have come
(D) comes

The word *if* indicates a conditional. Remember that a conditional sentence contains two clauses: a dependent clause beginning with *if*, and a main clause that answers the *if* clause.

This particular type of conditional is called a **future possible** condition because it describes a simple action that may, or may not, take place in the future, depending on whether Tony arrives.

In this type of conditional sentence, the main clause uses the future tense, and the *if* clause is in the *simple present*. This immediately narrows the choice down to choice (D) the only choice in the simple present tense.

Ⓐ Ⓑ Ⓒ ●

THE SENTENCE SHOULD READ:

Will you give this message to Tony if he comes?

Example III (Subordinate conjunctions)

We can tell Kathy when she ____________ from her trip.

(A) will return
(B) returns
(C) is returning
(D) returned

In the previous example you learned that the simple present tense is used after if in all future possible conditions. In the same way, the present tense is used after all subordinate conjunctions (*when, until, before, unless, as soon as, while,* etc.) when they are used to introduce clauses with a future meaning.

In this example Kathy will return from her trip and receive the news at a future time. The missing verb follows *when* and should be in the present tense. The correct answer is choice (B).

Ⓐ ● Ⓒ Ⓓ

THE SENTENCE SHOULD READ:

We can tell Kathy when she returns from her trip.

Example IV (Using the correct preposition)

The children usually play indoors __________ a rainy day.

(A) in
(B) on
(C) at
(D) while

Choosing the correct preposition is simple if you remember the general rules listed below.

Use *on* for:

Days of the week (on Monday/ on Saturdays)

Exact dates (on May 22nd/ on New Year's Day/ on the Fourth of July)

Particular kinds of day— answering the question "What kind of?" (on a sunny morning/ on windy nights)

Use *in* for:

Dates that mention only the month and/or year (in January/ in December, 1991/ in the year 2000)

Seasons (in summer/in the fall)

Parts of the day that answer the question "When?" (in the early morning/ in the afternoons)

Use *at* for:

Exact time (at midnight/ at five A.M.)

Official holidays or festivals when the exact day is not mentioned (at Christmas/ at Passover)

With *night* (at night)

Take another look at Example 4. It's telling us what kind of day, therefore the answer is choice (B), *on*.

Ⓐ ● Ⓒ Ⓓ

THE SENTENCE SHOULD READ:

The children usually play indoors on a rainy day.

Example V (Verbs of force or persuasion followed by that)

Steve's mom insisted that he __________ all his homework assignments before he went to his friend's house.

(A) to finish (C) finish
(B) finishing (D) finished

Certain verbs of force (*insist/ demand/ require*) or persuasion (*suggest/ recommend*) are followed by *that* + subject + **infinitive verb** (without **to**).

If you remember this, it becomes obvious that the correct answer is (C).

Ⓐ Ⓑ ● Ⓓ

THE SENTENCE SHOULD READ:

Steve's mom insisted that he finish all his homework assignments before he went to his friend's house.

NOW YOU TRY

Try the short practice exercises that follows. The sentences are similar to the examples in Day 4 Part 1 and should present no problems.

1. Omar will be able to go with us if he __________.

(A) is hurrying (C) hurries
(B) will hurry (D) hurried

Ⓐ Ⓑ Ⓒ Ⓓ

2. We will leave as soon as Lyn and Martin __________ here.

(A) will get (C) gets
(B) get (D) is getting

Ⓐ Ⓑ Ⓒ Ⓓ

3. The woman demanded that he __________ the house immediately or she would call the police.

(A) would leave (C) to leave
(B) is leaving (D) leave

Ⓐ Ⓑ Ⓒ Ⓓ

4. Since Bob always plays bridge __________ Saturday nights, I think it would be better to invite him over on Sunday.

(A) at (C) while
(B) in (D) on

Ⓐ Ⓑ Ⓒ Ⓓ

5. Professor Mackaill recommended that Laurie ____________ in British History.

(A) not to major
(B) wouldn't major
(C) not major
(D) isn't majoring

(A) (B) (C) (D)

6. I will let you know if he ____________ me.

(A) will call
(B) has called
(C) is calling
(D) calls

(A) (B) (C) (D)

7. I plan to go skiing in Denver __________ February. How about you?

(A) in
(B) on
(C) at
(D) while

(A) (B) (C) (D)

8. You've missed Elaine; she __________ home.

(A) is just leaving
(B) has just went
(C) has just been
(D) has just gone

(A) (B) (C) (D)

9. Wait here until Chuck __________.

(A) will call
(B) calls
(C) will have called
(D) is calling

(A) (B) (C) (D)

10. It often ______________ here in December.

(A) snows
(B) is snowing
(C) will snow
(D) will have snowed

Ⓐ Ⓑ Ⓒ Ⓓ

11. I insisted that he ______________ the police immediately.

(A) to call
(B) calling
(C) called
(D) call

Ⓐ Ⓑ Ⓒ Ⓓ

12. I won't go unless you ______________ too.

(A) goes
(B) went
(C) will go
(D) go

Ⓐ Ⓑ Ⓒ Ⓓ

13. We agreed to meet ______________ midnight on December 31st.

(A) in
(B) at
(C) on
(D) for

Ⓐ Ⓑ Ⓒ Ⓓ

14. I love to eat breakfast outside on the patio ______________ sunny mornings.

(A) in
(B) at
(C) on
(D) while

Ⓐ Ⓑ Ⓒ Ⓓ

15. If we ____________ enough money, we will go on vacation next summer.

(A) will save
(B) save
(C) will have saved
(D) are saving

Ⓐ Ⓑ Ⓒ Ⓓ

Check your answers. Refer back to the examples above if you have difficulties.

1. (C) see Example 2
2. (B) see Example 3
3. (D) see Example 5
4. (D) see Example 4
5. (C) see Example 5
6. (D) see Example 2
7. (A) see Example 4
8. (D) see Example 1
9. (B) see Example 3
10. (A) see Example 1
11. (D) see Example 5
12. (D) see Example 3
13. (B) see Example 4
14. (C) see Example 4
15. (B) see Example 2

Take a short break before going on to Part 2.

DAY 4

Part 2
Vocabulary Warm–Up

Today's vocabulary warm–up will be brief. During the past three days you have studied the importance of *base words* together with *prefixes* and *suffixes*. Today you will spend time reviewing to help you remember this information.

Choose the word needed to fill in the blank in the sentences below.

1. He stated that his decision to resign was ____________ and that nothing would persuade him to reconsider.

   (A) irresponsible
   (B) irreversible
   (C) unreasonable
   (D) informal

   Ⓐ Ⓑ Ⓒ Ⓓ

2. I was afraid there would be general ____________, but everyone liked the proposal.

   (A) despair
   (B) distress
   (C) disbelief
   (D) disagreement

   Ⓐ Ⓑ Ⓒ Ⓓ

3. The product did not turn out to be popular and was later ____________.

(A) disagreed
(B) disowned
(C) discontinued
(D) dissolved

Ⓐ Ⓑ Ⓒ Ⓓ

4. I ____________ my ability to learn to drive.

(A) mistake
(B) misled
(C) miscast
(D) mistrust

Ⓐ Ⓑ Ⓒ Ⓓ

5. The scandal has caused ____________ damage to my friend's reputation.

(A) irreparable
(B) inadequate
(C) inefficient
(D) insensible

Ⓐ Ⓑ Ⓒ Ⓓ

6. Communication with the space shuttle was lost for a short time, but was quickly ____________ .

(A) replanted
(B) refueled
(C) reestablished
(D) reformed

Ⓐ Ⓑ Ⓒ Ⓓ

7. Police surveillance proved ______________, and the suspect disappeared without a trace.

(A) unexpected
(B) inadequate
(C) illegal
(D) inexpensive

Ⓐ Ⓑ Ⓒ Ⓓ

8. The coach watched in ______________ as his team proceeded to lose the season's most important game.

(A) disbelief
(B) inability
(C) prejudice
(D) refreshment

Ⓐ Ⓑ Ⓒ Ⓓ

9. Your behavior was improper and totally ______________!

(A) disorganized
(B) untried
(C) unacceptable
(D) disinterested

Ⓐ Ⓑ Ⓒ Ⓓ

10. There has been much ______________ tension between the black and hispanic populations in that town.

(A) international
(B) interracial
(C) premature
(D) disorganized

Ⓐ Ⓑ Ⓒ Ⓓ

Check your answers below.

1 (B)	3 (C)	5 (A)	7 (B)	9 (C)
2 (D)	4 (D)	6 (C)	8 (A)	10 (B)

DAY 5

Part 1
Structure and Written Expression
(continued)

Today you will continue working on structure (incomplete sentences) found in Section 2 of the TOEFL test. Below are more examples of the kinds of sentences that may appear in the test.

Example VI (Adverb or adjective)

__________ this country was known as Ceylon but now it's called Sri Lanka.

(A) Origin
(B) Original
(C) Originates
(D) Originally

It's difficult to fill in a blank at the very beginning of a sentence. The simplest way to find out what is needed is to change the word order.

THE SENTENCE THEN READS:

This country was __________ known as Ceylon, but now it's called Sri Lanka.

The missing word would modify or add to the meaning of the verb *was known,* hence an adverb is needed. The only adverb among the answer choices is (D).

(A) (B) (C) ●

THE SENTENCE SHOULD READ:

Originally this country was known as Ceylon, but now it's called Sri Lanka.

Be Careful!

Sometimes you'll find an adverb has been placed before an adjective just to confuse you. A phrase like *very easy* does not mean the same as *easily*. It is still being used as an adjective. A sentence such as "He won the first set of the match *very easy*" is incorrect. It should read "He won the first set of the match *very easily*."

Example VII (Verb tense/Choice of verbs/Use of prepositions)

I'm pleased to meet you . Cliff ____________ so much about you.

(A) is telling me
(B) told to me
(C) has told me
(D) has said to me

First make sure you have the correct verb! Choice (D) is incorrect because the wrong verb is used. (Remember that *say* and *tell* have the same meaning but are used differently. The verb *tell* is used when the person to whom the words are spoken is mentioned.)

You now have the correct verb *tell*. Next, look at the prepositions. The verb tell is never followed by the preposition *to*. Therefore, the phrase *to me* is incorrect. Ignore choice (B).

The time sequence is also important. The speaker is talking now about an action that began in the past and has continued until now (*being told so much about the other person*). Therefore, the verb tense should look at the past from the present viewpoint—that is, the present perfect (*has* + **the past participle**).

Choice (C) is the correct answer.

Ⓐ Ⓑ ● Ⓓ

THE SENTENCE SHOULD READ:

I'm pleased to meet you. Cliff <u>has told me</u> so much about you.

Example VIII (Questions in indirect speech)

He asked his wife ____________ for her new dress.

(A) how much she paid
(B) how did she pay much
(C) how much she pays
(D) how she paid very much

Questions in indirect or reported speech can be confusing. There are several important points to remember. First, if the main verb in a sentence is in the past tense, the other verbs in the sentence must also be in the past tense. Choice (C) is incorrect because the verb is in the present tense.

Remember that a direct question (He asked, "How much did you pay?") becomes a simple statement of fact in reported speech. The subject now comes before the verb (*question word* + **subject** + **verb**).

Look at the choices. Ignore choice (B) and choice (D) because the word order is obviously incorrect: the words *how* and *much* should go together.

The remaining answer choice (A), is correct. The verb is in the past tense and follows the correct word order (**question words** *how much* + **subject** *she* + **verb** *paid*).

● (B) (C) (D)

THE SENTENCE SHOULD READ:

He asked his wife how much she paid for her new dress.

Example IX (First, second, third, etc...or last)

Janie was always the first student ____________ her work.

(A) finish
(B) to finish
(C) finished
(D) who finishes

Phrases that imply order such as *the first person*, the *last competitor* etc. are followed by *to* + **the infinitive.** This is not affected by the tense of the main verb. Therefore, the correct answer is choice (B).

(A) ● (C) (D)

THE SENTENCE SHOULD READ:

Jane was always the first student to finish her work.

Example X (Words often confused)

____________ it was raining heavily, we still went on the picnic.

(A) Despite
(B) In spite of
(C) Although
(D) Because of

First change the word order so that the blank does not occur at the beginning of the sentence. It now reads: We still left for our picnic ____________ it was raining heavily.

Next, consider the meanings of the choices available, since these are TOEFL test favorites. Notice that the missing word or phrase is followed by a subject and verb (. . . it was raining).

Look at Choice (D). *Because of* is always followed by a noun (e.g. *because of* the heavy rain). It implies direct cause and is quite different in meaning from the others.

Choices (A) and (B) have the same meaning, but both also need to be followed by a noun (e.g., *despite* the heavy rain; *in spite of* the heavy rain).

The remaining choice, (C), is correct. *Although* is always followed by a subject and verb. (Remember that *although, though* and *even though* are used in exactly the same way.)

(A) (B) ● (D)

THE SENTENCE SHOULD READ:

Although it was raining heavily, we still went to the picnic.

Note: Do not confuse these with the phrases *despite the fact that* and *in spite of the fact* , which are followed by a subject and verb.

MORE PRACTICE SENTENCES

1. I'm not sure how long Mr. Troyer plans to be out of town. He ____________ away since May.

(A) was
(B) will be
(C) will have been
(D) has been

Ⓐ Ⓑ Ⓒ Ⓓ

2. They decided to call their friends with the wonderful news, ____________ it was nearly two A.M.

(A) despite
(B) in spite of
(C) because
(D) even though

Ⓐ Ⓑ Ⓒ Ⓓ

3. I wasn't surprised to hear that Richard was the last runner ____________ the marathon.

(A) completed
(B) to complete
(C) completes
(D) who will complete

Ⓐ Ⓑ Ⓒ Ⓓ

4. Frank has a habit of always speaking ____________.

(A) very candid
(B) mostly candidly
(C) most candid
(D) candidly

(A) (B) (C) (D)

5. The second expedition ____________ the South Pole was led by Robert Falcon Scott.

(A) to reach
(B) that was reaching
(C) reached
(D) reach

(A) (B) (C) (D)

6. Professor Ford asked me ____________ my new class.

(A) how did I like
(B) how have I liked
(C) how much I liked
(D) how much I'd like

(A) (B) (C) (D)

7. We had fun on our vacation ____________ the dismal weather.

(A) although
(B) despite
(C) because
(D) even though

(A) (B) (C) (D)

8. She didn't tell me ___________.

(A) where did she live
(B) where is she living
(C) where was she living
(D) where she lived

Ⓐ Ⓑ Ⓒ Ⓓ

9. Mr. Hartung moved to Detroit in 1990 and ___________ there ever since.

(A) has lived
(B) will have lived
(C) lives
(D) is living

Ⓐ Ⓑ Ⓒ Ⓓ

10. Jere deserved to win because she played ___________.

(A) surprisingly good
(B) surprised
(C) surprisingly well
(D) surprising

Ⓐ Ⓑ Ⓒ Ⓓ

11. I don't know ___________ from here to Denver.

(A) how far is it
(B) how far it is
(C) how it is far
(D) how is it far

Ⓐ Ⓑ Ⓒ Ⓓ

12. I asked Steve when ____________ in town.

(A) would be he
(B) will he be
(C) is he
(D) he would be

Ⓐ Ⓑ Ⓒ Ⓓ

13. Trish is always the last guest ____________ at parties.

(A) arrive
(B) arrived
(C) to arrive
(D) who arrives

Ⓐ Ⓑ Ⓒ Ⓓ

14. Martina is an exceptionally ____________ driver.

(A) caringly
(B) carelessly
(C) carefully
(D) careful

Ⓐ Ⓑ Ⓒ Ⓓ

15. She went ahead and got married ____________ her parents disapproved.

(A) despite
(B) even though
(C) because of
(D) in spite of

Ⓐ Ⓑ Ⓒ Ⓓ

Check your answers below before taking a ten-minute break.

1. (D) see Example 7
2. (D) see Example 10
3. (B) see Example 9
4. (D) see Example 6
5. (A) see Example 9
6. (C) see Example 8
7. (B) see Example 10
8. (D) see Example 8
9. (A) see Example 7
10. (C) see Example 6
11. (B) see Example 8
12. (D) see Example 8
13. (C) see Example 9
14. (D) see Example 6
15. (B) see Example 10

DAY 5

Part 2
Vocabulary Building

Today you will examine the type of vocabulary items that appear in the last section of the TOEFL test. Don't worry about the actual exam format; that will be explained in detail on Day 8. Concentrate instead on reviewing the vocabulary items listed below.

It is impossible to try to memorize hundreds of new words in time for the exam. However, what you can do in the next few days, is review a limited number of items that may prove useful.

VERBS: Remember, it is always easier to learn new words in the context of a sentence. Read through the examples several times, substituting a different verb each time. All the verbs listed are acceptable synonyms.

Example I

The teacher	*scolded* *rebuked* *reprimanded* *chastised*	the noisy students.

Example II

Next week's French test has been	*called off.* *cancelled.*

Example III

Steve's contract was	*ended* *terminated* *concluded*	without any warning.

Example IV

The other students	*laughed at* *ridiculed* *mocked* *made fun of*	the new child.

Example V

We	*disapprove of* *condemn* *denounce*	cruelty to animals.

NOW IT'S YOUR TURN

Among the words listed below, find one or more acceptable synonyms among the words listed below to replace the words underlined in the following sentences.

(a) denounced	(e) canceled
(b) reprimanded	(f) scolded
(c) made fun of	(g) ended
(d) concluded	(h) mocked

_____ 1. The woman rebuked her assistant for neglecting her duties.

_____ 2. The school carnival was called off at very short notice.

_____ 3. He terminated his business partnership before leaving town.

_____ 4. The unkind girl always ridiculed her younger sister.

_____ 5. They all condemned the man's outrageous behavior.

Now check your answers below. Refer back to the examples if you need to.

1. **rebuked**	(b) reprimanded	(f) scolded
2. **called off**	(e) canceled	
3. **terminated**	(d) concluded	(g) ended
4. **ridiculed**	(c) made fun of	(h) mocked
5. **condemned**	(a) denounced	

FURTHER EXAMPLES

Continue working through these examples of the kinds of verb you may encounter in the vocabulary section of TOEFL test. As before, read each sentence several times, substituting a different verb each time. All are acceptable synonyms.

Example VI

The professor has agreed to *put off* the test until next week.
postpone
delay
defer

Example VII

I *admitted* that I had made a mistake.
acknowledged
conceded
confessed

Example VIII

The accident *took place* last night.
happened
occurred

Example IX

The hostage was *freed* after two days of negotiations.
released
liberated

Example X

Doug said he would *go with* / *accompany* / *escort* Jane to the prom.

MORE PRACTICE SENTENCES

Among the words listed below find one or more acceptable synonyms to replace the words underlined in the following sentences.

(a) acknowledged
(b) took place
(c) released
(d) escorted
(e) confessed
(f) deferred
(g) liberated
(h) postponed
(i) occurred

_____ 1. The prisoner was freed after serving three years in jail.

_____ 2. He finally admitted he had stolen the money.

_____ 3. Who accompanied you to the party?

_____ 4. I want to know what happened after I left.

_____ 5. The announcement will be delayed for a week.

Now check your answers below. Refer back to the examples if you need to.

1. **freed**	(c) released	(g) liberated
2. **admitted**	(a) acknowledged	(e) confessed
3. **accompanied**	(d) escorted	
4. **happened**	(b) took place	(i) occurred
5. **delayed**	(f) deferred	(h) postponed

DAY 6

Part 1
Structure and Written Expression
(continued)

PART B
Written Expression (Find the mistake)

Here you will read a sentence in which four words or phrases are underlined. You have to find the one that is wrong and fill in the oval next to the corresponding letter on your answer sheet. Only one is word or phrase is incorrect.

Remember that the parts of the sentence not underlined are correct. Use them! They can help you find which of the underlined words or phrases is wrong. For example, if the subject of the sentence is not underlined and it is singular, you know that its verb should also be singular. See (A) in the sentence below:

She fully <u>understand</u> <u>that</u> she will have <u>to retake</u> the exam <u>at</u> a

A B C D

a later date.

Here the singular subject (*she*) needs a singular verb (*understands*).

She fully **<u>understands</u>** that she will have to retake the exam at a later date.

Read all the examples that follow, and make sure you understand the process for pinpointing the incorrect word or phrase. Often it's simply a case of knowing what to look for. Each example has been chosen to help you do just that.

Note: The TOEFL test only requires you to chose the incorrect word or phrase. You are not expected to correct it. The corrected version is given here at the end of each example only for your benefit.

Example I (Verbs)

Mrs. Hughes said she had see two boys break into the house

A **B** **C**

earlier that evening.

D

Always check first to see if any verbs or verb parts are underlined —that's where you should focus. In this case, you'd go straight to (A) and (B).

One glance at (A) shows that said is correct, so take a close look at (B). The past perfect tense is formed by using the past tense of the helping verb *have* + the past participle. The past participle of the verb *see* is *seen*.

(A) ● (C) (D)

THE SENTENCE SHOULD READ:

Mrs. Hughes said she **had seen** two boys break into the house earlier that evening.

Be on the lookout for incorrect past participles in compound tenses or in the passive (examples: The letter was *wrote* by my best friend). They are common errors on this part of the test.

Example II (Apostrophe 's)

Spain's Costa del Sol has long been well-known for it's
A B C D

sunny climate.

If there are no underlined verbs to worry about, focus on an apostrophe (or even on a word that looks as though it might need an apostrophe). In this example pay attention to (A) and (D).

Many students find apostrophes challenging, but they're really quite simple if you remember the following:

It's is really a shortened form of *it is.*

Possessive pronouns (*its, his, hers, yours, theirs, and ours*) never have an apostrophe.

In this example (A) is the correct possessive form of the noun *Spain.* (D), however, is incorrect because it is the possessive form and is not acting as a shortened form of *it is.*

● (B) (C) (D)

THE SENTENCE SHOULD READ:

Spain's Costa del Sol has long been well-known for **its** sunny climate.

Example III (Adverbs and adjectives)

Unfortunately, Rose doesn't sing as sweet as her two sisters do.
A B C D

Always check underlined adverbs and adjectives; they are often misused in the TOEFL test. Take a look at (C) in the example above. Does Rose sing sweet or sweetLY? There is no need to look any further for the mistake in this sentence!

(A) (B) ● (D)

THE SENTENCE SHOULD READ:

Unfortunately, Rose doesn't sing as **sweetly** as her two sisters do.

Example IV (Singular or plural subjects)

That pile of papers need to be thrown away immediately!
A B C D

As usual, first take a look at the underlined verbs or verbs—in this case (B) and (C). Always check the subject to see if it agrees, with the verb. Remember, a singular subject needs a singular verb; a plural subject should have a plural verb.

Is *pile* or *papers* the subject of the verb *need* (B)? If you are unsure, simply remove the phrase *of papers* and try the sentence again. It now reads:

That pile need to be thrown away immediately.

Pile is singular and should be followed by a singular verb.

(A) ● (C) (D)

THE SENTENCE SHOULD READ:

That pile of papers **needs** to be thrown away immediately!

NOTE: The TOEFL will often try to confuse you by filling the space between the subject and its verb with plural phrases, as in this sentence with the phrase of papers. Beware!

Example 5 (More singular and plural problems)

Each (A) of the actors recited the lines (B) they (C) knew best (D).

Be alert the moment you see indefinite pronouns (*each, anybody, nobody, everyone, someone, neither, etc.*) in a sentence. These pronouns are singular. Always check to see that any pronouns that refer back are also singular.

In this example, the real subject of the sentence, *each*, has been separated from the verb by the plural phrase *of the actors*. This is done to confuse you. Remember, *each* and other words like it are singular. Therefore (C) is incorrect.

(A) (B) ● (D)

THE SENTENCE SHOULD READ:

Each of the actors recited the lines **he** knew best.

Don't forget that *all, any, some* and *none* are four indefinite pronouns that may be singular or plural, depending on how they are used in the sentence. For example:

Some of the money **was** missing.

Some of the students **were** absent.

NOW IT'S YOUR TURN

If you worked through these examples, you should have no problems with the following exercises.

1. Its very obvious to everyone that Tim's parents disapprove of
A **B** **C** **D**
his marriage to Cindy.

Ⓐ Ⓑ Ⓒ Ⓓ

2. Annie answered the interviewer's questions so skillful that
A **B** **C**
she was immediately hired.
D

Ⓐ Ⓑ Ⓒ Ⓓ

3. At the time of his arrest, the man had drank nearly twice the
A **B** **C** **D**
legal limit.

Ⓐ Ⓑ Ⓒ Ⓓ

4. None of the planes was taking off on that foggy morning
A **B** **C**
in the fall.
D

Ⓐ Ⓑ Ⓒ Ⓓ

5. The book found in the hallway was neither Mark's nor her's.
A **B** **C** **D**

Ⓐ Ⓑ Ⓒ Ⓓ

6. I know that Dennis expect (A) his math teacher to fail (B) him this semester, but I think his exam grade will pull (C) him through (D).

(A) (B) (C) (D)

7. The number of students interested (A) in signing up for Beginning Spanish 1 have (B) almost (C) doubled this semester thanks to (D) the new professor.

(A) (B) (C) (D)

8. Bill felt (A) unhappily (B) when he heard about (C) his brother's (D) success.

(A) (B) (C) (D)

9. Any student wishing (A) to take Dr. Ford's (B) course in linguistics next semester need (C) to sign up by Wednesday (D).

(A) (B) (C) (D)

10. The cost (A) of some seasonal (B) fruits and vegetables (C) have risen (D) sharply due to an unexpected demand.

(A) (B) (C) (D)

11. I believe its time government officials took measures to
A B
limit their spending in the area.
C D

(A) (B) (C) (D)

12. Neither of the students involved in the fight were allowed
A B
to leave the campus until the dispute was settled.
C D

(A) (B) (C) (D)

13. Ilse can hardly speak English, unlike her sister who already
A B C
speaks it good.
D

(A) (B) (C) (D)

14. Frank said he never would have went to the meeting if he
A B
had known it would be so boring.
C D

(A) (B) (C) (D)

15. The group of students planning to go away on the ski trip
A B
have to obtain written permission from their parents.
C D

(A) (B) (C) (D)

Now check your answers below and take a short break. Then read on.

1. (A) see Example 2
2. (C) see Example 3
3. (C) see Example 1
4. (A) see Example 5
5. (D) see Example 2
6. (A) see Example 1
7. (B) see Example 4
8. (B) see Example 3
9. (C) see Example 5
10. (D) see Example 4
11. (A) see Example 2
12. (B) see Example 5
13. (D) see Example 3
14. (B) see Example 1
15. (C) see Example 4

DAY 6

Part 2
Vocabulary Building

Today you will continue to review useful vocabulary items for the last section of the TOEFL test. This time the emphasis is on nouns.

Again it is best to review word meanings in the context of a sentence. Read through the following examples several times, substituting a different noun each time. All the nouns listed are acceptable synonyms.

Example I

The *result* of my accident was a broken leg.
consequence
outcome
conclusion

Example II

What are your *standards* when judging essays?
criteria

Example III

Employees should take their *complaints* to the management.
grievances
gripes

Example IV

Television has become boring because of the *lack* of good programs.
scarcity
dearth

Example V

Many were unaware of the *importance* of the AIDS epidemic.
magnitude
gravity
extent

NOW IT'S YOUR TURN

Among the words listed below find one or more acceptable synonyms to replace the underlined words in the following sentences.

(a) consequence
(b) complaints
(c) dearth
(d) magnitude
(e) criteria
(f) extent
(g) outcome
(h) grievances
(i) scarcity
(j) gravity

_____ 1. The <u>importance</u> of the situation should not be underestimated.

_____ 2. I get tired of listening to everybody's <u>gripes</u>.

_____ 3. Harvard University has high <u>standards</u> for admission.

_____ 4. The <u>lack</u> of quality players on the team was apparent to all.

_____ 5. The <u>result</u> of the quarrel was an end to our friendship.

Check your answers below. Refer back to the examples if you need to.

1. **<u>importance</u>** (d) magnitude (j) gravity (f) extent
2. **<u>gripes</u>** (b) complaints (h) grievances
3. **<u>standards</u>** (e) criteria
4. **<u>lack</u>** (c) dearth (i) scarcity
5. **<u>result</u>** (a) consequence (g) outco'

ADDITIONAL EXAMPLES

Continue working through the following examples of the types of noun you may encounter in the TOEFL vocabulary section. As before, read each sentence several times, substituting a different noun each time. All are acceptable synonyms.

Example VI

At the *height* of its power, Britain ruled much of the world.
peak
zenith

Example VII

The Iraqi invasion of Kuwait proved to be a *disaster* for many people.
calamity
catastrophe

Example VIII

The *threat* of forest fires is constant during the dry season.
danger

Example IX

Police are continuing their *hunt* for those who witnessed the accident.
search

Example X

An insect passes through several *stages* of development.
phases

MORE PRACTICE SENTENCES

Among the words listed below, find one or more acceptable synonyms to replace the words underlined in the following sentences.

(a) peak
(b) danger
(c) phases
(d) zenith
(e) calamity
(f) hunt
(g) catastrophe

_____ 1. The prospectors were willing to spend years in their search for gold.

_____ 2. He won Wimbledon at the height of his tennis career.

_____ 3. The threat of war hung over the country.

_____ 4. The rainy season proved to be a disaster for my country.

_____ 5. There are various stages in the development of a good tennis player.

Check your answers below. Refer back to the examples if you need to.

1. **search** (f) hunt
2. **height** (a) peak (d) zenith
3. **threat** (b) danger
4. **disaster** (e) calamity (g) catastrophe
5. **stages** (c) phases

DAY 7

Part 1
Structure and Written Expression
(continued)

Today you will be looking at more examples of the kinds of sentences you may come across in the Written Expression part of Section 2. Remember that these examples are useful because they show you the type of error to look for. They are not presented in any special order; all are important and helpful.

Example VI (More about pronouns)

Most of his friends felt **(A)** that Hank shouldn't **(B)** blame hisself **(C)** for what **(D)** happened.

When compound pronouns (*himself, herself, themselves* etc.) are underlined in a sentence it pays to take a closer look at them. Often, as in the example above, you'll find the pronoun is misspelled. Here (C) is incorrect.

(A) (B) ● (D)

THE SENTENCE SHOULD READ:

Most of his friends felt that Hank shouldn't blame **himself** for what had happened.

Example VII (Check your compound tenses)

I feel Jim would of (**A**) done well (**B**) on the exam if he had studied (**C**) more (**D**).

It may sound like *would of*, but remember that the modal is always written *would have.* (A) is incorrect.

● (B) (C) (D)

THE SENTENCE SHOULD READ:

I feel Jim **would have** done well on the exam if he had studied more.

Example VIII (How long?)

She has been (**A**) a vegetarian since (**B**) many years, but her husband still (**C**) enjoys eating (**D**) red meat.

Now is a good time to make sure you understand the difference in meaning and use of the words *since, for, from, to* and *ago.* If you see one of these words underlined in a TOEFL sentence, check it.

Since is used to **pinpoint** the **exact** time in the past when an action began. This action is open-ended: it has continued up until the present and is still going on.

Example: She has lived here *since* January.

For is used to describe the length of time during which an action took place.

Example: He lived in London *for* six months.

From . . . to is used to describe the length of time during which an action took place when both start and finish are known.

Example: He was in college *from* 1970 *to* 1974.

Ago is used only with the past tense. It refers to an action that took place and was completed in the past.

Example: He went to Chicago two years *ago*.

If you look back at the example sentence, you will note that *since* is used incorrectly. The phrase describes how long she has been a vegetarian. It does not refer to the point of time in the past when she became a vegetarian. Therefore, (B) is incorrect.

(A) ● (C) (D)

THE SENTENCE SHOULD READ:

She has been a vegetarian **for** many years, but her husband still enjoys eating red meat.

Example IX (Who, which or that)

The high school principal (**A**) is the person which (**B**) deals with (**C**) this type of problem (**D**).

Relative pronouns (*who, which, that*) can present problems. If you see them underlined in a sentence, check to see if they are used correctly.

> Remember:
>
> *Who* refers to people.
>
> *That* refers to people or objects.
>
> *Which* refers to animals, objects, or collective nouns.

In the example above, *which* refers to the principal and is therefore incorrect.

(A) ● (C) (D)

THE SENTENCE SHOULD READ:

The high school principal is the person **who** deals with this type of problem.

NOTE: *Whose* and *whom* can also be tricky.

Whose is the possessive form of *who* (*Whose* book is this?). This form should not be confused with *who's* which is the shortened form of who is (*Who's* coming to the party tonight?)

Whom is used as the direct object of the verb (*Whom* did Rose call?) and as the object of a preposition (To *whom* was she speaking?)

Example X (Does it match?)

I <u>really</u> don't think that <u>neither</u> the boy <u>or</u> his friend <u>is</u> to blame.
A **B** **C** **D**

It's easy to read through the sentence so quickly that you fail to realize that simple, everyday expressions don't match up. Look out for mismatchings in *either* . . . or/and *neither* . . . *nor*. These cannot be interchanged. *Either* has to be followed by or; neither has to be followed by *nor*. Also remember that *neither* . . . . *nor* <u>cannot</u> be used with a negative verb. Therefore (B) is incorrect.

(A) ● (C) (D)

THE SENTENCE SHOULD READ:

I reallly don't think that **<u>either</u>** the boy or his friend is to blame.

EVEN MORE PRACTICE

1. You would never (A) know that Ulf has been studying (B) English (C) since (D) only two years.

(A) (B) (C) (D)

2. I realize I should of called (A) the police as soon as I knew (B) that something was (C) wrong (D).

(A) (B) (C) (D)

3. I didn't (A) know that the Smiths lived in (B) Detroit since (C) 1982 to 1986 (D).

(A) (B) (C) (D)

4. Many Europeans (A) now view theirselves (B) as part (C) of the middle class (D).

(A) (B) (C) (D)

5. The child didn't (A) recognize the men which (B) entered the house late (C) that (D) night.

(A) (B) (C) (D)

6. Luckily, neither the boy or his father was injured in the crash.
A B C D

(A) (B) (C) (D)

7. With who do you plan to attend next week's reception?
A B C D

(A) (B) (C) (D)

8. There was little he could do hisself to ease the pain.
A B C D

(A) (B) (C) (D)

9. I have no idea whose coming to live next door.
A B C D

(A) (B) (C) (D)

10. If they had known she was stranded at the airport, they would of gone to get her themselves.
A B C D

(A) (B) (C) (D)

11. Coach Gabriel has (A) some last minute travel information for (B) the teams who (C) are playing (D) in the tournament.

Ⓐ Ⓑ Ⓒ Ⓓ

12. They soon realized that they hadn't given (A) theirselves (B) enough time to complete (C) their (D) science project.

Ⓐ Ⓑ Ⓒ Ⓓ

13. I don't think (A) that either (B) Pam nor (C) Joe deserves (D) the prize.

Ⓐ Ⓑ Ⓒ Ⓓ

14. Did you know (A) that Hank's (B) daughter worked (C) in the family travel business since (D) two years?

Ⓐ Ⓑ Ⓒ Ⓓ

15. He realizes (A) now that he should of (B) spent more time with his children when they were growing (C) up (D).

Ⓐ Ⓑ Ⓒ Ⓓ

Check your answers below, then take a ten-minute break before starting on Part 2.

1. (D) see Example 8
2. (A) see Example 7
3. (C) see Example 8
4. (B) see Example 6
5. (B) see Example 9
6. (C) see Example 10
7. (B) see Example 9
8. (D) see Example 6
9. (C) see Example 9
10. (B) see Example 7
11. (C) see Example 9
12. (B) see Example 6
13. (C) see Example 10
14. (D) see Example 8
15. (B) see Example 7

DAY 7

Part 2
Vocabulary Building

Today you will continue to review the type of vocabulary items which may appear in the last section of the TOEFL® test. This time you will study a selection of useful adjectives.

Always review word meanings in the context of a sentence. Read through the examples several times, substituting a different adjective each time. All the adjectives listed are acceptable synonyms.

Example I

The snake they all thought was *poisonous* turned out *harmless*.

venomous / *innocuous.*

Example II

The president made a *brief and clear* statement.

succinct
concise
terse

Example III

It didn't take much to make the *hot-headed* man lose control.

hot-tempered
irascible
choleric
irritable

Example IV

No one can stop the *relentless* passage of time.
inexorable
unyielding

Example V

I felt hurt by his *unfriendly* comments.
adverse
hostile
antagonistic

NOW IT'S YOUR TURN

Find one or more acceptable synonyms among the words listed below to replace the words underlined in the following sentences.

(a) innocuous	(f) succinct
(b) laconic	(g) irascible
(c) choleric	(h) unyielding
(d) inexorable	(i) antagonistic
(e) unfriendly	(j) terse

_____ 1. The manager gave a concise report of the meeting.

_____ 2. His remarks seemed harmless.

_____ 3. He was relentless in his desire for revenge.

_____ 4. I find her hostile attitude very difficult to deal with.

_____ 5. A hot-tempered nature can get you into a lot of trouble!

Now check your answers below. Refer back to the examples if you need to.

1. **concise**	(b) concise	(f) succinct (j) terse
2. **harmless**	(a) innocuous	
3. **relentless**	(d) inexorable	(h) unyielding
4. **hostile**	(e) unfriendly	(i) antagonistic
5. **hot-tempered**	(c) choleric	(g) irascible

FURTHER EXAMPLES

Now continue working through examples of the kinds of adjective you may come across in the vocabulary section. As before, read each sentence several times substituting a different adjective each time. All are acceptable synonyms.

Example VI

Our *curious* neighbor was determined to know what had happened.
inquisitive
prying

Example VII

Her *hopeful* nature means that she always looks on the bright side.
optimistic
sanguine

Example VIII

He feared that someone would learn of their *secret* meetings.
clandestine
surreptitious

Example IX

What we need is a *workable* plan.
viable
feasible
practicable

Example X

Bad eggs have a *disagreeable* odor.
unpleasant
objectionable
offensive

MORE PRACTICE SENTENCES

Among the words listed below, find one or more acceptable synonyms replace the words underlined in the following sentences.

(a) offensive
(b) sanguine
(c) curious
(d) viable
(e) objectionable
(f) prying
(g) feasible
(h) clandestine
(i) disagreeable
(j) surreptitious

_____ 1. Juliet's <u>secret</u> meetings with Romeo soon led to their marriage.

_____ 2. <u>Inquisitive</u> people should learn to mind their own business!

_____ 3. The plan is a <u>practicable</u> one and will be put into action right away.

_____ 4. I found the movie extremely <u>unpleasant</u> and left shortly after it started.

_____ 5. My family always tries to view life with an <u>optimistic</u> attitude.

Check your answers below. Refer back to the examples if you need to. Then you will be finished for today.

1.	**secret**	(h) clandestine	(j) surreptitious
2.	**inquisitive**	(c) curious	(f) prying
3.	**practicable**	(d) viable	(g) feasible
4.	**unpleasant**	(a) offensive	(e) objectionable
		(i) disagreeable	
5.	**optimistic**	(b) sanguine	

Section 2 Summary

Structure and Written Expression

This section lasts twenty-five minutes, it has a total of 40 questions, and it is divided into two parts.

PART A: Structure

Choose the word or phrase that will best complete a given sentence.

PART B: Written Expression

Indicate which of several underlined parts in a sentence is incorrect.

DAY 8

Part 1
Vocabulary and Reading Comprehension
(total time: 45 minutes)

Today you will begin working on the third section of the TOEFL® test.

PART A
Vocabulary (Choose the Synonyms)

You will read a sentence in which a word or phrase has been underlined. Below you will find four possible answers. You then choose the word or phrase that could replace what has been underlined without changing the meaning of the sentence. In other words, you have to find a synonym.

Your Strategy—What You Need To Know

This part of the TOEFL test is a straightforward test of vocabulary knowledge. In most cases you will know the synonym or you won't. It is probable, however, that the vocabulary building program will have improved your chances of knowing the answer.

The subjects of the sentences won't be of much help to you because all the choices will seem to fit into the structure of the sentence (for example, the choices will all be adverbs, or verbs, or whatever part of speech is needed).

It is very important not to waste time on the Vocabulary part. You need to budget your time and work through these questions quickly in order to save as much time as possible for the Reading Comprehension passages that will follow.

Do not waste time reading the general directions. Start working right away. Go straight to the underlined word in the sentence and look for its synonym among the answer choices. Reading the sentence will not provide much help, and it will use up valuable time.

Be ruthless. If you find that you don't know the meaning of the underlined word or phrase, use your **guess** choice and move on! (Remember to use the same letter each time you do this.)

During the past three days, the second part of your study sessions have aimed at building your knowledge of synonyms. Now take a look at some examples of the types of sentences you will come across using vocabulary items already reviewed.

Example I

Union leaders throughout the country have <u>denounced</u> the government's new policy.

(A) despised
(B) condemned
(C) supported
(D) upheld

The best choice is (B) because *condemned* does not change the meaning:

Union leaders throughout the country have **<u>condemned</u>** the government's new policy.

(A) ● (C) (D)

Example II

He was fully aware of the extent of the problem.

(A) criteria
(B) consequences
(C) magnitude
(D) outcome

The best choice is (C) because *magnitude* does not change the meaning:

He was fully aware of the **magnitude** of the problem.

(A) (B) ● (D)

Example III

The attorney's concise summation impressed the jury.

(A) innocuous
(B) reliable
(C) relentless
(D) succinct

The best choice is (D) because *succinct* does not change the meaning.

The attorney's **succinct** summation impressed the jury.

(A) (B) (C) ●

NOW IT'S YOUR TURN

The exercises below follow the format of the Vocabulary section of the TOEFL test. Try to work through each question as quickly as you can. Remember, context is of no help here. Don't waste any time trying to figure out the meaning. Work at maximum speed.

1. The hearing was postponed until a later date.

   (A) cancelled
   (B) retried
   (C) deferred
   (D) acknowledged

   A B C D

2. The result of the peace talks is still not known.

   (A) magnitude
   (B) outcome
   (C) zenith
   (D) dearth

   A B C D

3. Everyone lived in fear of the irascible old tyrant.

   (A) questioning
   (B) terse
   (C) innocuous
   (D) choleric

   A B C D

4. Playing Hamlet at the Old Vic theater marked the <u>zenith</u> of this fine actor's career.

(A) termination
(B) peak
(C) dearth
(D) quest

Ⓐ Ⓑ Ⓒ Ⓓ

5. The guard was publicly <u>reprimanded</u> for failing to follow orders.

(A) derided
(B) challenged
(C) rebuked
(D) commended

Ⓐ Ⓑ Ⓒ Ⓓ

6. He was <u>relentless</u> in his demand for justice.

(A) triumphant
(B) inexorable
(C) irritable
(D) innocuous

Ⓐ Ⓑ Ⓒ Ⓓ

7. The peace negotiations were <u>concluded</u> last week.

(A) terminated
(B) deferred
(C) instigated
(D) resumed

Ⓐ Ⓑ Ⓒ Ⓓ

8. His venomous remarks ruined the entire evening.

(A) innocuous (C) poisonous
(B) benign (D) flattering

(A) (B) (C) (D)

9. His startling theories were ridiculed for many years.

(A) derided (C) supported
(B) challenged (D) ignored

(A) (B) (C) (D)

10. Despite many misgivings, I confess you were right to act as you did.

(A) suggest (C) deny
(B) reiterate (D) acknowledge

(A) (B) (C) (D)

11. The opening performance was called off without explanation.

(A) postponed (C) brought forward
(B) cancelled (D) anticipated

(A) (B) (C) (D)

12. He was worn out by his mother-in-law's endless <u>complaints</u>.

(A) nagging
(B) remarks
(C) suggestions
(D) requests

Ⓐ Ⓑ Ⓒ Ⓓ

13. The sudden bushfire proved <u>disastrous</u> to the life of the village.

(A) unacceptable
(B) constructive
(C) inexorable
(D) catastrophic

Ⓐ Ⓑ Ⓒ Ⓓ

14. He <u>admitted</u> defeat in the election.

(A) denied
(B) contested
(C) conceded
(D) spurned

Ⓐ Ⓑ Ⓒ Ⓓ

15. All prisoners of war were <u>freed</u> after the ceasefire.

(A) imprisoned
(B) released
(C) interrogated
(D) sentenced

Ⓐ Ⓑ Ⓒ Ⓓ

Check your answers below. If you had problems with the vocabulary items listed, it means that you need to go back and review the second part of Days 5, 6, and 7.

1.	postponed	(C) deferred
2.	result	(B) outcome
3.	irascible	(D) choleric
4.	zenith	(B) peak
5.	reprimanded	(C) rebuked
6.	relentless	(B) inexorable
7.	concluded	(A) terminated
8.	venomous	(C) poisonous
9.	ridiculed	(A) derided
10.	confess	(D) acknowledge
11.	called off	(B) cancelled
12.	complaints	(A) nagging
13.	disastrous	(D) catastrophic
14.	admitted	(C) conceded
15.	freed	(B) released

Take a break before beginning Part 2.

DAY 8

Part 2
Vocabulary Building

Part 2 of today's study session will complete your vocabulary review for Section 3 of the TOEFL test. This time you will look at a selection of useful adverbs.

Use the same method as before. Read through the examples several times, substituting a different adverb each time. All the adverbs listed are acceptable synonyms.

Example I

I *often* have lunch with Marge, but I see her sister only *rarely.*
frequently — *occasionally.*
regularly — *seldom.*

Example II

He found the homework assignment *especially* difficult.
particularly

Example III

The children have been *quite* well-behaved all day.
relatively
comparatively

Example IV

He drove his car into the tree *on purpose.*
deliberately.
intentionally.

Example V

By the time we got there, *nearly* everybody had already gone.
almost
practically
virtually

NOW IT'S YOUR TURN

Among the words listed below, find one or more acceptable synonyms to take the place of the words underlined in the following sentences.

(a) often
(b) seldom
(c) virtually
(d) comparatively
(e) practically
(f) occasionally
(g) particularly
(h) intentionally
(i) frequently
(j) quite
(k) nearly
(l) on purpose

_____ 1. It's <u>relatively</u> warm for this time of year.

_____ 2. Attorneys said that she had <u>deliberately</u> destroyed all the evidence.

_____ 3. <u>Almost</u> everyone I know showed up at the surprise party.

_____ 4. It was <u>especially</u> nice of you to remember my birthday.

_____ 5. You should visit your dentist <u>regularly</u>.

_____ 6. We <u>rarely</u> eat at expensive restaurants.

Check your answers below. Refer back to the examples if you need to.

1. **relatively**	(d) comparatively,
	(j) quite
2. **deliberately**	(h) intentionally,
	(l) on purpose
3. **almost**	(c) virtually,
	(e) practically,
	(k) nearly
4. **especially**	(g) particularly
5. **regularly**	(a) often,
	(i) frequently
6. **rarely**	(b) seldom,
	(f) occasionally

FURTHER EXAMPLES

Continue to work through the following examples of the kinds of adverbs you may encounter in the vocabulary section of the TOEFL test. As before, read each sentence several times, substituting a different adverb each time. All are acceptable synonyms.

Example VI

I mentioned the party *accidentally* and spoiled the surprise.
inadvertently
untentionally

Example VII

This area consists *mainly* of desert.
chiefly
mostly
largely
for the most part
principally

Example VIII

From time to time I go to Boston to visit my grandmother.
Every so often
Every now and then
Once in a while
Periodically

Example IX

I sat down and answered his letter *immediately.*
right away.
at once.

Example X

The principal remained *firmly* opposed to the students' request.
inflexibly
steadfastly
immovably
adamantly
unyieldingly

MORE PRACTICE SENTENCES

Among the words listed below, find one or more acceptable synonyms to take the place of the words underlined in the following sentences.

(a) unintentionally
(b) every so often
(c) adamantly
(d) immediately
(e) at once
(f) unyieldingly
(g) every now and then
(h) inadvertently
(i) from time to time
(j) largely
(k) inflexibly
(l) chiefly
(m) for the most part
(n) immovably
(o) mostly
(p) directly
(q) firmly
(r) principally
(s) periodically

_____ 1. I accidentally picked up your textbook thinking it was mine.

_____ 2. He said he would deal with the matter right away.

_____ 3. His clients are mainly from South America.

_____ 4. He has always stood steadfastly in the way of progress.

_____ 5. Since my best friend moved away, I see her only once in a while.

Check your answers below. Refer back to the examples if you need to. Then finish for today.

1. **accidentally**	(a) unintentionally	(h) inadvertently
2. **right away**	(d) immediately	(e) at once
3. **mainly**	(j) largely	(l) chiefly
	(m) for the most part	(o) mostly
	(r) principally	
4. **steadfastly**	(c) adamantly	(f) unyieldingly
	(k) inflexibly	(n) immovably
	(q) firmly	
5. **once in while**	(b) every so often	
	(g) every now and then	(s) periodically
	(i) from time to time	

DAY 9

Part 1
Vocabulary and Reading Comprehension (continued)

PART B
Reading Comprehension

The remainder of this section involves reading a number of passages followed by several questions. You choose the best answer to each question from the four choices given.

Your Strategy—What You Need To Know

This part of the TOEFL test is quite different from the preceding vocabulary questions. Here context is most important. Some of the passages will seem difficult but don't let this worry you. All the information needed to answer the questions will be either stated or implied in the reading passage. You are not expected to have any prior knowledge of the subject.

You will also notice that the number of questions following each passage may vary. Again, don't let this worry you. The fact that a passage has more questions does not mean that it's more difficult. Be prepared for questions that ask you to find the main idea of the passage by choosing a suitable title. Other questions will require more specific answers. Be prepared.

Students who are slow readers tend to feel apprehensive about this section. The time factor is always a problem in any test, and because of it you need to distinguish different types of reading.

The TOEFL test is neither the time nor the place for in-depth reading. Instead, you should make full use of skimming and scanning techniques. Each of these has its own method and purpose. It should reassure you to know that most people automatically use these techniques in everyday life without even knowing they are doing so.

Skimming involves quickly running your eyes over a passage in order to get the gist or general idea of the content. This is not as difficult as it sounds. You already do this when you preview a long article in a magazine to see if it's worth reading or when you check what kinds of pizza are on the menu at your local fast food place. Skimming is part of everyday life.

Pay particular attention to the first and last paragraphs because these often summarize the main idea of the passage. Also read the first and last sentences in each paragraph in order to find the topic sentences.

Scanning is a helpful technique when you need to find a specific answer. Scanning is what you do when you look up a number in the telephone book or locate a particular event or battle in a history book.

Scanning means quickly moving your eyes across a line or down a page. You don't need to read every word. Simply remember the key word or phrase in the question and be on the lookout for it. Once you have located the information you need, slow down and read more carefully.

The Reading Comprehension section of the TOEFL tests your ability in a number of ways. If the test were not timed, you would first read the passage in order to get acquainted with it. Then you would look at the questions and begin locating the answer to each of them. But the TOEFL simply does not allow you enough time to work this way.

In this situation you will find the following strategies useful:

Always read the questions first. Look quickly through all of them. It's quite likely that you'll find the answer to one question while looking for another. This will also allow you to see if there's a question at the end asking for the main idea.

1. Next re-read each question one by one and scan the passage until you find the keyword or phrase from the question. The answer is sure to be nearby.
2. Remember to use skimming when a question asks about the general content of the passage.
3. Above all, relax. It's not as difficult as it sounds. Work through the sample passages below to see what is involved.

PASSAGE 1: QUESTIONS 1–4

You will read:

The Shakers are officially referred to as the United Society of Believers in Christ's Second Appearing. The name "Shakers" comes from the way they "danced" in church. They would jump about in an attempt to shake the evil from their bodies. As time went on they started to organize specific dances, believing that God gave them arms and legs to use in worshipping Him. Eager to find more time for worship, they continually improved their systems of heating, cooling, lighting, and housekeeping.

The Shakers are famous for their inventions and skill at making furniture. Even a partial list of their inventions is astounding. They invented the clothespin, the flat-sided broom, the waterwheel, and the alarm clock. They created kitchen utensils, such as an appliance for paring, coring, and quartering apples. They are also credited with the first circular saw, the threshing machine, the pea sheller, and the first aquaduct to carry water directly to the kitchen.

Many types of furniture we use today are copied from the Shakers' original designs. Shaker furniture was pleasing to the eye but designed more for function than beauty. The Shakers wanted to be comfortable while they worshipped. For example, they made chairs with ladder-type backs, using horrizontal rungs instead of vertical ones. They fashioned the first chairs with woven wicker seats and backs. They also built sturdy tables, sewing desks and cupboards.

(Janet R. Swinton and William J. Agopsowicz, *Read and Respond* (Los Angeles, Calif.: Roxbury Publishing Company, 1987), pp. 40—41).

1. According to the passage, how did the Shakers acquire their name?

(A) From the abbreviation of their full name.
(B) From their founder's name.
(C) From the household appliances they invented.
(D) From the way they jumped or danced in church.

Ⓐ Ⓑ Ⓒ Ⓓ

2. Which of the following is not mentioned in the passage as a Shaker invention?

(A) The alarm clock.
(B) The pea sheller.
(C) The butter churn.
(D) The threshing machine.

Ⓐ Ⓑ Ⓒ Ⓓ

3. Why did the Shakers make chairs with ladder-type backs, using horizontal rungs instead of vertical?

(A) For beauty.
(B) For comfort.
(C) For durability.
(D) For easy repair.

Ⓐ Ⓑ Ⓒ Ⓓ

4. The Shakers continually made household improvements so that

(A) They would have more time for worship.
(B) They would attract more followers.
(C) They would have more free time.
(D) They would encourage young people to remain.

Ⓐ Ⓑ Ⓒ Ⓓ

PASSAGE 2: QUESTIONS 5-6

You will read:

A migraine is a severe headache caused by a narrowing of blood vessels in the brain, followed by an enlargement of these vessels. Before the pain begins, some people see bright spots or feel tingling sensations in their legs and arms. This is followed by intense pain, sensitivity to light, and often nausea. As the early symptoms fade away, an intense throbbing headache follows. A migraine comes on quickly and may last a day or two. It may occur repeatedly or very rarely. There seem to be many causes of migraines. This type of headache may be brought on by stress, drinking alcohol, smoking, particular foods or chemicals, or changes in the daily routine. A tendency toward having migraines may be passed on through families. Many medicines have been used to relieve these headaches, with some success. At present there is no cure.

(Getchell, Pippin, and Varnes, *Perspectives on Health* (Lexington Mass.: D.C. Heath and Company, 1992 p. 247).

5. Which of the following is not a symptom of a migraine?

    (A) Nausea.
    (B) Tingling sensation in arms and legs.
    (C) Feeling of lightheadedness.
    (D) Sensitivity to light.

    (A) (B) (C) (D)

6. The author states that

    (A) most people experience a migraine headache in the course of their lives.
    (B) the tendency to migraine headaches may be hereditary.
    (C) migraine headaches can be completely relieved through medication.
    (D) migraine headaches rarely last longer than a couple of hours.

    (A) (B) (C) (D)

PASSAGE 3: QUESTIONS 7–9

You will read:

Top officials are now calling lead the No. 1 environmental threat to children. The new concern is based on evidence that far smaller doses of lead than previously believed can harm children. Studies conducted over the last ten years suggest that ingesting the lead equilvalent of three granules of sugar a day can slow development and make children less intelligent. If that's true, even the dust created by a lead-painted window rubbing against its sill can be toxic to children, and old networks of lead water pipes pose serious hazards. This makes lead a health risk in many homes, from crumbling inner city tenements to suburban houses that were once thought to be relatively safe from lead. U.S. public health officials estimate that 3 million tons of leaded paint still line the interiors of 57 million private American homes or nearly 60 percent of the housing stock.

Source: ("Lead and Your Kids," from NEWSWEEK, February 17, 1992,

7. The passage states that small doses of lead in children can result in

   (A) mental imbalance and mood swings.
   (B) severe headaches and possible eye disorders.
   (C) mental retardation.
   (D) restricted growth and reduced intelligence.

   Ⓐ Ⓑ Ⓒ Ⓓ

8. There is evidence that children may be harmed by ingesting

   (A) three granules of sugar a day.
   (B) the lead equivalent of three granules of sugar over 10 years.
   (C) the lead equivalent of three granules of sugar a day.
   (D) three granules of lead paint dust.

   Ⓐ Ⓑ Ⓒ Ⓓ

9. How many homes are now a lead hazard according to US public health officials?
   (A) 3 million.
   (B) 57 million.
   (C) 60 million.
   (D) No reliable figures are available.

Ⓐ Ⓑ Ⓒ Ⓓ

PASSAGE 4: QUESTIONS 10-12

You will read:

Worried about your cholesterol level? An American company has developed a cassette-size, do-it-yourself testing unit that measures the total cholesterol in blood. "The test takes about 15 minutes and has an accuracy comparable to instrumented tests," claims . . . (the) public healthcare company based in Sunnyvale, California. The product . . . is available by prescription in the United States and other countries and sold over the counter in Italy. . . . The product does not determine the level or the ratio of high-and-low density lipoproteins in the blood which is important in evaluating the health of some patients . . . A tip: if the cholesterol reading is over 200, additional testing is recommended. Price: about $15.

Source: ("A Blood Test," from NEWSWEEK, April 20, 1992.

10. The passage is mainly concerned with.
    (A) the importance of regularly checking your cholesterol level.
    (B) different means of checking your cholesterol level.
    (C) a newly developed do-it-yourself cholesterol test.
    (D) finding the best way to check your cholesterol level.

Ⓐ Ⓑ Ⓒ Ⓓ

11. Which of the following does the American product not do?
   (A) Measure the total cholesterol in blood.
   (B) Give readings of over 200.
   (C) Evaluate the health of the patient.
   (D) Determine the level of high-and-low-density lipoproteins.

Ⓐ Ⓑ Ⓒ Ⓓ

12. You do not need a doctor's prescription to buy the product in
   (A) the United States.
   (B) California.
   (C) Italy.
   (D) EEC countries.

Ⓐ Ⓑ Ⓒ Ⓓ

PASSAGE 5: QUESTIONS 13–15

You will read:

Some day, maybe, the countries of the European Community will share a common currency. Future ECU users can get a head start with Monopoly's® new European Edition. The $42 game, which has just hit stores in five EC nations, comes with heaps of ECU play money emblazoned with all sorts of European monuments. Not that Parker Brothers plans to drop the various national versions it has marketed for decades; the French edition alone sells 350,000 copies a year.

Source: ("Return to Go and Collect 2,000 ECUs," from NEWSWEEK, April 20, 1992,

13. What is the best title for this passage?
   (A) European Common Currency.
   (B) Monopoly ® Goes European.
   (C) European Money Market.
   (D) Getting Ready for Europe.

Ⓐ Ⓑ Ⓒ Ⓓ

14. The new board game is played with
   (A) currencies from five EC nations.
   (B) an imaginary EC currency.
   (C) a currency based on the American dollar.
   (D) ECU currency.

Ⓐ Ⓑ Ⓒ Ⓓ

15. This new version of Monopoly® is now available in
   (A) all EC countries.
   (B) five EC countries.
   (C) the United States.
   (D) France.

Ⓐ Ⓑ Ⓒ Ⓓ

Check your answers below and take a short break. Then read on.

1. (D)
2 (C)
3. (B)
4. (A)
5. (C)
6. (B)
7. (D)
8. (C)
9. (B)
10. (C)
11. (D)
12. (C)
13. (B)
14. (D)
15. (B)

DAY 9

Part 2
More Practice

Part 2 will provide you with more practice in reading comprehension.

PASSAGE 6: QUESTIONS 16-17

You will read:

Chemical secretions are used by many animals as signals. Such secretions are called pheromones. These chemicals influence the behavior of other members of the same species. Pheromones can act as sex attractants. The female silkworm moth releases a pheromone so strong that it attracts males from a distance as great as three kilometers. Gypsy moths, cockroaches, and many other insects produce pheromones that act as sex attractants.

Source: (Schraer and Stoltze, *Biology the Study of Life* (Englewood Cliffs, N.J.: Prentice-Hall Inc., 1991, p. 804.)

16. Which insect uses a pheromone to attract males from distances of up to 3 kilometers?
    (A) Cockroach.
    (B) Gypsy moth.
    (C) Silkworm moth.
    (D) Silkworm.

A B C D

17. The passage does not mention that pheromones are

(A) sex attractants.
(B) used for camouflage.
(C) used as animal signals.
(D) chemical secretions.

(A) (B) (C) (D)

PASSAGE 7: QUESTIONS 18–19

You will read:

It may have been the costliest criminal conviction in history. To catch Manuel Antoñio Noriega, the U.S. government had to invade Panama with 27,000 troops, resulting in the deaths of 23 U.S. soldiers and several hundred Panamanians. Operation Just Cause was expensive, too: it cost American taxpayers $164 million. And to convict the former dictator, prosecutors made deals with more than a dozen drug traffickers, dropping charges, offering reduced sentences, and allowing some to keep their fortunes from selling cocaine.

Source: ("Noriega: How the Feds Got Their Man," from NEWSWEEK, April 20, 1992, © Newsweek, Inc. All rights reserved. Reprinted by permission).

18. The purpose behind Operation Just Cause was

(A) to spend $164 million of the American taxpayers' money.
(B) to bring a dozen cocaine drug traffickers to justice.
(C) to send 27,000 American troops overseas.
(D) to invade Panama and capture General Noriega.

(A) (B) (C) (D)

19. How did prosecutors ensure Noriega was convicted?

(A) By offering to reduce his sentence for a plea of guilty.
(B) By making deals with drug dealers.
(C) By allowing him to keep the money made from selling cocaine.
(D) By making deals with the government of Panama.

(A) (B) (C) (D)

PASSAGE 8: QUESTIONS 20–23

You will read:

During the 1200's, Marco Polo, an Italian traveler and merchant, made a long overland trip from Europe to eastern Asia. After Marco Polo returned to Europe, the story of what he had seen in China was published in a book. Marco Polo had a great deal to tell Europeans about Chinese culture. He described the ship canals, wide, tree-lined roadways, and a communications system made up of messengers on horseback. He also told of gunpowder, paper, and magnetic compasses - all Chinese inventions unknown to Europe at the time. He also explained how the Chinese burned "black stone," or coal, to warm their homes and bathwater. Europeans of Marco Polo's day burned only wood or charcoal as heating fuel.

Many people in Europe read or heard about the new and wonderful things Marco Polo had seen. Not everyone believed what he reported. Yet his report marked the beginning of a new and strong European interest in trade with Asia. Over the next several centuries, the exchange of goods between European and Asian traders grew steadily.

Source: (Charles F. Gritzner, *World Geography* (Lexington Mass: D.C. Heath and Company, 1989 pp. 143–44).

20. According to the passage, how did Marco Polo's fellow Europeans learn about Chinese culture?

(A) Chinese books became available in Europe.
(B) Chinese goods became available in Europe.
(C) Marco Polo published a series of letters to his uncle.
(D) Marco Polo published a book about his travels.

Ⓐ Ⓑ Ⓒ Ⓓ

21. According to Marco Polo, what did the Chinese use to heat their homes and bathwater?

(A) Coal.
(B) Wood.
(C) Charcoal.
(D) Gunpowder.

Ⓐ Ⓑ Ⓒ Ⓓ

22. Which of the following is not mentioned as a Chinese invention?

(A) Paper.
(B) Magnetic compasses.
(C) Gunpowder.
(D) Charcoal.

Ⓐ Ⓑ Ⓒ Ⓓ

23. What happened as a result of Marco Polo's report?

(A) Europeans wanted to visit China.
(B) Europeans became interested in trading with Asia.
(C) He persuaded wealthy patrons to finance subsequent trips.
(D) He established new sea routes to Southwest Asia.

Ⓐ Ⓑ Ⓒ Ⓓ

PASSAGE 9: QUESTIONS 24-28

You will read:

Hibernating bears are able to defy some basic rules of mamalian physiology, research has shown. Five months of inactivity would lead to disastrous bone thinning in humans, but leaves bears unharmed. Although bears do not move their large muscles for more than 100 days, they actually increase their lean body mass in the den. And while bears do not urinate during their months of hibernation, their bodies show no buildup of urea, a toxic waste of protein metabolism normally eliminated by the kidneys.

A group of scientists studying the internal chemistry of hibernating bears say they have identified the secret of their survival: recycling. Hibernating bears seem to be able to make use of bone degradation products to build new bone and urinary wastes to make protein. The researchers hope to use chemicals from the bear to treat humans suffering from osteoporosis, in which the bones waste away, and from kidney failure, in which life-threatening urinary toxins accumulate.

Source: ("Tapping the Secrets of Sleeping Bears," *International Herald Tribune*, April 23, 1992).

24. According to the passage, hibernating bears make use of urinary wastes to

    (A) drastically lower their body temperatures.
    (B) maintain nutritional needs.
    (C) make protein.
    (D) build new bone.

Ⓐ Ⓑ Ⓒ Ⓓ

25. What would happen to the human body if it remained inactive for a period of several months?

(A) The bones would thin down and become brittle.
(B) Toxic wastes would not be eliminated.
(C) The body would recycle bone degradation products.
(D) Lean body mass would increase.

Ⓐ Ⓑ Ⓒ Ⓓ

26. What is urea?

(A) A bone degradation product.
(B) A protein produced from toxic waste products.
(C) A toxic waste product usually eliminated by the kidneys.
(D) A chemical produced by the bear during hibernation.

Ⓐ Ⓑ Ⓒ Ⓓ

27. How long do bears hibernate?

(A) Three months.
(B) Four months.
(C) Five months.
(D) Six months.

Ⓐ Ⓑ Ⓒ Ⓓ

Check your answers below. Then go back and repeat scanning techniques where necessary to see where you went wrong. Then you are finished for today.

16. (C)	18. (D)	20. (D)	22. (D)	24. (C)	26. (C)	28. (A)
17. (B)	19. (B)	21. (A)	23. (B)	25. (A)	27. (C)	

Section 3 Summary

Vocabulary and Reading Comprehension

This section lasts 45 minutes.

It has a total of 60 questions.

It is divided into two parts.

PART A: Vocabulary

Choose the word or phrase which could replace the underlined section of a sentence.

PART B: Reading Comprehension

Read several passages and choose the correct answers to the questions that follow.

DAY 10

Part 1
Final Review

The Ten Day Plan is almost at an end. Today you will review the exam format for one last time.

Your Strategy—What You Should Know By Now

In many ways, taking the TOEFL test is like taking part in an exciting sport. You need to be flexible and able to vary your shots according to the situation.

Budget Your Time For Success

Be alert all the time. When you're in that exam room, think of nothing but the TOEFL!

You have already worked through each individual part of the exam. Now take another look at the complete format.

Section 1: Listening Comprehension

(50 questions in forty minutes)

Don't waste time listening to the general directions. Make sure you know exactly what you have to do in this part of the TOEFL test so you can use the time allotted for general directions to start reading ahead.

Stop reading as soon as you hear the question number on the tape. Remember you will hear each sentence, conversation, or talk just **one** time. Listen carefully.

The tape will control the speed at which you work. During the short pause, select your answer. If you don't know the answer use your pre-planned **"guess"** letter. Never leave a question unanswered, and never make a wild guess.

Read the next four answer choices if you finish before the 12–second pause is up, but remember, to stop reading as soon as you hear the next question number on the tape. LISTEN.

Part A: You will hear a single sentence. Choose the answer that says the same thing in a different way.

Part B: You will hear a fairly short conversation, followed by a question. You then choose the most suitable answer. Try to remember who says what (for example, at a party the woman wants to leave early, the man would prefer to stay).

Pay attention to any clues that tell you where the dialogue is taking place (in a travel agency; at the dentist; in a drugstore) or the relationship between the speakers (doctor and patient; teacher and student; bank teller and client).

Listen to the tone of voice. Is the speaker angry, pleased, or asking a favor? Are certain words or phrases being stressed?

Part C: Here the conversations and selections will sound more formal and impersonal. You need to retain more information in order to answer several questions that follow. But remember, it is not a test of memory.

You should try to preread the answer choices before you hear the talk. Make sure you know exactly what you have to do in this part of the exam. Read ahead while the general directions are being given.

Preread the answers to the first two or three questions. It will mean that you will scan the answers more quickly after the selection. You will then be able to preread answer choices to the next question. Try to stay ahead of the tape.

Remember that sometimes the answer choices themselves can help. If three of the four choices are mentioned on the tape, it is likely that the fourth will be the answer you're looking for.

Most important of all, **never** attempt to read while you are listening to the tape. Always listen carefully to what is said.

SECTION 2: STRUCTURE AND WRITTEN EXPRESSION

(40 questions in twenty–five minutes)

You're in charge now. The fact that the test now deals with written English means that **you** dictate the pace. Don't rush–try to work steadily. Make sure you read **all** the possible answer choices.

Don't waste time reading the general directions. Make sure you know exactly what you have to do in this part of the TOEFL test so you can use the time allotted for directions to begin the test.

Part A: Structure (Incomplete Sentences)–choose the word or phrase necessary to complete the missing part of the sentence. Grammar is important.

Part B: Written Expression (Spot the Mistake) Four parts of a sentence will be underlined. You choose the one that is incorrect.

Remember that all parts of a sentence are related. Use the parts that are not underlined (and therefore correct) to help you understand what might be wrong.

Section 3
Vocabulary and Reading Comprehension

(60 questions in forty– five minutes)

How you manage your time is also vital in this section. Don't waste time reading the general directions. Make sure you know exactly what you have to do in this part of the TOEFL test so you can use this time to start on the test.

Plan to finish Part A as quickly as possible. If you don't know an answer, **guess**. (Remember, always use the same letter each time you guess.)

Spend more time on Part B. Think about what is required. Make full use of **skimming** and **scanning** techniques.

Part A: Vocabulary—Choose the word or phrase that can replace what is underlined in the sentence without altering the meaning. Don't waste any time. Don't read the whole sentence, concentrate instead on the underlined word. Keep in mind what you learned about prefixes and suffixes.

Part B: Reading Comprehension—Choose the correct answer to the questions which follow the reading passages. Avoid in–depth reading. Use **skimming** and **scanning** techniques.

Quickly read through **all** the questions before you start. Then deal with each individual question. Identify the **key** words or phrases in the question, then locate the answer in the reading passage. Be prepared to choose a suitable title for a passage or to state the main idea.

If necessary take the time to re-read this final review until you are sure you understand what is involved in every section of the TOEFL test. You should have no doubts about what you have to do. Today's Part 2 will check whether or not you do.

DAY 10

Part 2
Take the Mini TOEFL

Finish the Ten Day Plan by working through a mini session of the TOEFL test. Before you begin, read the section on Answering Practice Questions in your copy of the *TOEFL® Bulletin of Information* published by ETS. Pay particular attention to the directions given because they are similar to those on the test.

The directions in the mini–exam below are very brief. They are meant to act only as a guide. By now you should not need directions. You should <u>know</u> what is required in each section of the test.

Note: You will need the accompanying cassette.

SECTION 1: Listening Comprehension

Do <u>not</u> press PAUSE until you come to the end of Section 1.

Part A: Choose the sentence that **restates** the sentence you hear.

1. (A) Bob couldn't solve Alison's math problem.
   (B) Alison needed Bob's help right away.
   (C) Alison was not speaking to Bob.
   (D) Bob didn't know what was wrong with Alison.

(A) (B) (C) (D)

2. (A) Chuck's wife asked him to pick up his suit from the cleaners.
   (B) Chuck asked his wife to get his suit from the cleaners.
   (C) Chuck's wife wanted him to take his suit to the cleaners.
   (D) Chuck told his wife that his suit needed to go to the cleaners.

Ⓐ Ⓑ Ⓒ Ⓓ

3. (A) Dennis lent $50 to each of his sisters.
   (B) Dennis borrowed $50 from each of his sisters.
   (C) Dennis gave money to his sister.
   (D) Dennis' sisters each loaned him $50.

Ⓐ Ⓑ Ⓒ Ⓓ

4. (A) Celeste's dress isn't gorgeous.
   (B) Celeste isn't wearing a gorgeous dress to the prom.
   (C) Celeste is gorgeous but her dress is not.
   (D) Celeste's dress is gorgeous.

Ⓐ Ⓑ Ⓒ Ⓓ

Part B: Choose the letter that best answers the question you will hear after each conversation.

5. (A) Richard hasn't decided yet.
   (B) No, he's too busy.
   (C) Yes, even though he's busy.
   (D) The woman hasn't been able to ask him yet.

Ⓐ Ⓑ Ⓒ Ⓓ

6. (A) He answers the phone.
   (B) He works for the manager.
   (C) He is the manager.
   (D) He is an accountant.

Ⓐ Ⓑ Ⓒ Ⓓ

7. (A) She wants the man to fix it now.
   (B) She wants the repairman to fix it.
   (C) She wants to buy a new VCR.
   (D) She wants to feel happier.

Ⓐ Ⓑ Ⓒ Ⓓ

Part C: Choose the correct answers to the questions you will hear after the passage.

8. (A) Insufficient protein.
   (B) Insufficient phosphorus.
   (C) Insufficient calcium.
   (D) Insufficient magnesium.

Ⓐ Ⓑ Ⓒ Ⓓ

9. (A) 300 per day.
   (B) 315 per day.
   (C) 50 percent more.
   (D) 15 percent more.

Ⓐ Ⓑ Ⓒ Ⓓ

10. (A) A baby with weak bones.
    (B) An underweight baby.
    (C) A premature baby.
    (D) A malformed baby.

Ⓐ Ⓑ Ⓒ Ⓓ

TURN OFF THE TAPE

SECTION 2: Structure and Written Expression

Part A: Structure

Choose the word or phrase needed to complete the sentence.

1. I __________ here for over an hour and certainly don't plan to leave now!

   (A) have been staying
   (B) will have waited
   (C) have been waiting
   (D) will wait

   Ⓐ Ⓑ Ⓒ Ⓓ

2. She refused to tell me __________ her new dress.

   (A) where she buy
   (B) where did she buy
   (C) where was she buying
   (D) where she bought

   Ⓐ Ⓑ Ⓒ Ⓓ

3. We arrived on time __________ the delay due to fog.

   (A) although
   (B) despite
   (C) because of
   (D) even though

   Ⓐ Ⓑ Ⓒ Ⓓ

Part B: Written Expression

Find the underlined part of the sentence which is **incorrect**.

4. He has never felt more happier than he feels right now.
   A: never — B: more happier — C: feels — D: right now

   (A) (B) (C) (D)

5. The girl's mother realized it was broke as soon as she saw it.
   A: girl's — B: was broke — C: as soon as — D: she

   (A) (B) (C) (D)

6. It's obvious that they blame theirselves for what happened.
   A: It's — B: theirselves — C: for — D: happened

   (A) (B) (C) (D)

7. Don't you agree that Lorraine would of gotten a better seat if she had arrived earlier?
   A: Don't — B: would of gotten — C: better — D: had arrived

   (A) (B) (C) (D)

8. It's ridiculous to say you don't know whose responsible!
   A: It's — B: to say — C: don't know — D: whose

   (A) (B) (C) (D)

SECTION 3: Vocabulary and Reading Comprehension

Part A: Vocabulary

Select the word or phrase that could best **replace** the underlined word(s).

1. He was totally unaware of the seriousness of his situation.

   (A) consequences
   (B) gravity
   (C) criteria
   (D) outcome

   Ⓐ Ⓑ Ⓒ Ⓓ

2. A hot-tempered person would never be able to cope with the job.

   (A) nervous
   (B) disorganized
   (C) tactless
   (D) irascible

   Ⓐ Ⓑ Ⓒ Ⓓ

3. I anticipate that there will be problems with this matter.

   (A) foresee
   (B) admit
   (C) deny
   (D) concede

   Ⓐ Ⓑ Ⓒ Ⓓ

4. He took his complaint to the labor union and won.

(A) request
(B) grievance
(C) report
(D) findings

Ⓐ Ⓑ Ⓒ Ⓓ

5. Losing the final match proved disastrous for the team.

(A) disappointing
(B) unexpected
(C) disheartening
(D) catastophic

Ⓐ Ⓑ Ⓒ Ⓓ

Part B: Reading Comprehension

1. Choose the best answers to the questions that follow the passages below.

Consider some statistics on life and death in America:

• The infant–mortality rate for African-Americans, 17.7 deaths per 1,000 births, is more than double the average for whites. It's higher than the rate for Malaysia.

• Black children are three times more likely than whites to live in a single-parent household; 43.2 percent of all African-American children live in poverty.

• African-Americans now account for 28.8 per cent of US AIDS cases. Blacks comprise 52 percent of women with the disease, and black children represent 53 percent of all pediatric AIDS cases.

• Homicide is now the leading cause of death for African-American males between the ages of 15 and 34. Nearly half of all US murder victims are black.

• In 1989, 23 percent of all African-American men aged 20 to 29 were either in prison or on probation or parole. By one study, one fifth of all black males between 15 and 34 now have criminal records.

Source: ("Losing Ground," from NEWSWEEK, April 6, 1992,© Newsweek, Inc. Reprinted by permission).

6. According to the passage, the infant-mortality rate for blacks is

   (A) 17.7 percent higher than for whites.
   (B) less than the rate for Malaysia.
   (C) over twice the average for whites.
   (D) over twice the average in Malaysia.

(A) (B) (C) (D)

7. How many of all U.S. murder victims are black?

   (A) One in three.
   (B) Almost half.
   (C) Half.
   (D) One fifth.

(A) (B) (C) (D)

8. According to one study, how many black males between the ages of 15 and 34 now have been in trouble with the law?

   (A) 5 percent.
   (B) 20 percent.
   (C) 23 percent.
   (D) 43 percent.

(A) (B) (C) (D)

2. Ever wonder how much water you use when taking a shower? About 35 gallons. That may be a meaningless statistic to some, but in many parts of the world, water usage is a very serious issue. Hoping to enhance the public's awareness of excess water use—and make a little money, besides—a California company is selling the "world's first compact consumer water meter." The Water Watch is a simple plastic gauge that attaches to either a showerhead or a garden hose and graphically displays the number of gallons used (up to 50 gallons). The product . . . can be reset after each use. Price: $15.

Source: ("Saving Gallons," from NEWSWEEK©, February 24, 1992, Newsweek, Inc. All rights reserved. Reprinted by permission).

9. What does the Water Watch actually do?

   (A) Reduces excess water use.
   (B) Saves on water bills.
   (C) Stores excess water.
   (D) Measures water consumption.

Ⓐ Ⓑ Ⓒ Ⓓ

10. The maximum number of gallons the Water Watch will display is

   (A) 15.
   (B) 34.
   (C) 50.
   (D) endless.

Ⓐ Ⓑ Ⓒ Ⓓ

11. The company marketing the product hopes to

(A) prompt the public to use less water.
(B) make a profit.
(C) both of the above.
(D) neither of the above.

Ⓐ Ⓑ Ⓒ Ⓓ

Check your answers below, then read the Afterword.

Section 1: Listening Comprehension

Part A	1 (D)	2 (B)	3 (A)	4 (D)
Part B	5 (D)	6 (C)	7 (B)	
Part C	8 (C)	9 (A)	10 (B)	

Section 2: Structure and Written Expression

Part A	1 (C)	2 (D)	3 (B)	
Part B	4 (B)	5 (B)	6 (B)	7 (B)
	8 (D)			

Section 3: Vocabulary and Written Expression

Part A	1 (B)	2 (D)	3 (A)	4 (B)	5 (D)
Part B	6 (C)	7 (B)	8 (B)		
	9 (D)	10 (C)	11 (C)		

Afterword

You're all set! You're as ready as you'll ever be. Here is some last-minute advice to ensure that everything goes smoothly.

BEFORE THE EXAM

• Be sure to get plenty of sleep the night before the TOEFL® Test. You will need to be rested and alert for a long period of time. There is no rest break during the test!

• The exam may begin very early in the morning. Make sure you know exactly **when** you have to be at the test center. Allow plenty of time to find out where to report. Avoid being late or having to rush!

• You will not be allowed to leave the room once the test begins. Make sure you have enough time to drink water, eat a snack, or visit the bathroom. Remember that no food or drink will be allowed into the exam room and that includes gum and candy!

• Come prepared. Bring your admission ticket and necessary documentation for admission. Check the **WHAT TO TAKE TO THE TEST CENTER** section of your *TOEFL® Bulletin*—it's there to help. Make sure you have **everything** you need the day **before** the test.

• Bring the right equipment. You will need two sharpened (number 2 or HB) pencils, a clean eraser that works well, and a pencil sharpener (just in case). You may wear a watch, but remember—no beepers or alarms are allowed.

IN THE EXAM ROOM

• Follow the test supervisor's instructions **at all times**.

• Try to sit near the speakers. You want to make sure you hear **everything**.

• Do **not** read the directions.

• Make sure you **read** or **work** only on the section of the test being administered. Do not read ahead or go back to another section of the test later on.

• Do **not** mark or make notes on the test booklet. If you are taking the TWE® Test or essay section of the exam, the test supervisor will give directions on where you may make notes.

• Be sure to complete the answer sheet correctly. Fill in the oval that matches the answer you have chosen.

Remember that each question has only **one** answer. If you wish to change your answer, make sure you **completely** erase your previous answer.

• Make sure you answer all the questions on the test. If you don't know the answer, **guess**. But remember, always use the same letter each time you guess.

• If the worst happens and you find you've made a terrible mistake, raise your hand and inform the test supervisor. If you discover you've skipped a line so all your answers are in the wrong place, **don't** even try to start erasing and correcting your mistakes. Raise your hand and ask for help!

• Stop working when time is called. That means **you**, even if you're sitting way at the back of the room and think you're out of sight. If you continue writing this will be considered to be cheating.

• Finally, **never ever** attempt to cheat in **any** way. You'll get caught. Keep your eyes on your own test.

GOOD LUCK!

APPENDIX 1

What is the TWE® Test?

The Test of Written English® (TWE)® is offered with the TOEFL several times each year. Check in your *TOEFL® Bulletin of Information* for these dates. You will be given thirty minutes in which to write a 200–300 word essay on a stated topic.

Don't let the idea of an essay frighten you. The TWE® score will be listed separately on a scale of 1–6 (six being the highest) and will **not** affect your TOEFL score.

You will not have a choice of topic, but then, neither are you expected to have any special knowledge of the topic. Besides, imagine how much time students would waste making up their minds if they were given a choice of subject. This way it's easy—you just do it!

The good news is that you **will** be allowed to jot down a few useful notes to help you plan your essay. Listen to your test supervisor's directions and be sure to use only the space provided for this. Be brief–you won't have time to work on a draft of the essay. However, you **do** have time to write a few basic notes that will hold your essay together.

If you are asking yourself how on earth you can write a 200–300 word essay in just half-an-hour, read on.

Your Strategy—What You Need To Do

Candidates will usually be asked to compare and contrast different arguments. This may involve discussing opposite views to a question and expressing your own opinion on the subject. (For example, what are the arguments for and against capital punishment, and where do you stand on this?)

The question may require you to interpret information given on a simple graph or chart. This is actually easier, as all the facts you need are provided for you. The actual format of the essay remains the same.

Remember, you are **not** expected to have any prior knowledge of the topic, but you **are** expected to answer the question. Don't get side-tracked onto something else that interests you or your essay will receive no score.

Half-an-hour isn't long, but it's long enough **if** you budget your time carefully. It's vital that you spend the first 7–10 minutes reading the instructions and **thinking** about the topic. Jot down a few notes while you're thinking to keep you on track. Restate the question in your own words so you know **exactly** what is required.

Never try to save time by rushing into the actual writing of the essay. Anyone can misread the question and end up writing an essay that has nothing to do with the assigned topic. It's easily done, so beware.

Organization is most important if you want to produce a well–developed essay. How do you organize? Make sure your argument is balanced. Try to devote roughly the same amount of space to both sides of the argument. (In the example mentioned above, you would explain the arguments **for** and **against** capital punishment.)

Next, you develop your essay by **supporting** your main statements or topic sentences. It is not enough merely to state your own personal opinion. You will need to explain **why** you think as you do. (For example, **why** do those who support capital punishment think it's a good idea? **why** do those against it think it won't work?) Jot down two or three supporting details under **FOR** (+) and the same under **AGAINST** (–). A word or phrase is all that is needed.

The Five Paragraph Essay

Follow a simple essay format. Aim at producing a **five–paragraph** essay with approximately 50–60 words per paragraph. It may sound difficult, but you'll be pleasantly surprised at how easy it is.

Paragraph 1

This is the introduction to your essay. Make sure that you start the first paragraph with a clear **thesis statement** that narrows down the topic and immediately tells the reader what the essay will be about. The thesis statement should restate the question in your own words.

Follow your thesis statement with four **topic sentences**. That is, develop your thesis statement into main areas. The last of these topic sentences should express your own opinion **and** serve as a conclusion.

Your first paragraph will then consist of **five** sentences and follow the format given below:

I. (a) Thesis Statement (restates and narrows down topic)
(b) Topic Sentence (develops the thesis statement)
(c) Topic Sentence (develops the thesis statement)
(d) Topic Sentence (develops the thesis statement)
(e) Concluding topic sentence (expresses personal opinion)

If you follow this simple format, you will find that once you've written the first paragraph, the rest of the essay will be easy.

Remaining paragraphs

When you reach the second paragraph of the essay, simply begin by repeating a key word or phrase from the second sentence in your introductory paragraph (topic sentence b) or, if you're really short of time just repeat the sentence. Then write a further three or four sentences to support this topic sentence, as shown below:

II. (b) Topic Sentence
Supporting sentence
Supporting sentence
Supporting sentence
Supporting sentence

The remaining paragraphs are developed in the same way. Take the third sentence from your introductory paragraph (topic sentence c) to begin your third paragraph. Then develop the paragraph with supporting details. Do the same with the fourth and fifth paragraphs.

III. (c) Topic Sentence
Supporting sentence
Supporting sentence
Supporting sentence
Supporting sentence

IV. (d) Topic Sentence
Supporting sentence
Supporting sentence
Supporting sentence
Supporting sentence

V. (e) Concluding topic sentence
Supporting sentence
Supporting sentence
Supporting sentence

If you follow the format above, you will find that you are able to write a highly structured five–paragraph essay in the 30 minutes allotted. The fact that you repeat the topic sentences and then support them will ensure that your essay is organized and well developed.

NOW YOU TRY

The outline below applies the five paragraph format to arguments for and against capital punishment. Time yourself to see how long it takes.

First, think about the question and jot down key words and phrases.

<u>Capital Punishment</u>

FOR +	AGAINST –
deterrent effect	human life is sacred
justice: eye for an eye	won't bring back victim
removes danger to society	law can make mistakes
avoids prison expense	prison should be for life

Next, spend time carefully writing your introductory paragraph. It can make or break your essay. A sample thesis statement is given below.

Write the remaining topic sentences for the introductory paragraph. Make sure that they can all be supported by 3-4 sentences in later paragraphs.

(a) Some people are convinced that capital punishment is the only way to deal with murder, while others argue that the taking of any human life is to be condemned.

(b) ______________________________

(c) ______________________________

(d) ______________________________

(e) ______________________________

Read through what you have written to ensure that it "flows." Remember, if your first paragraph is good, the rest will follow.

LAST WORD

Your copy of the *TOEFL® Bulletin of Information* will provide you with sample topics similar to those on this section of the exam. Spend ten minutes thinking about each one and practice jotting down the key words and phrases that structure your essay. Then try writing an introductory paragraph with a clear thesis statement and relevant topic sentences.

Tapescript

DAY 1: Listening Comprehension Part A

Example 1

Man: The two of us finished the painting job in just four hours–half the time it would have taken me to do it by myself.

Example 2

Woman: The game started at six o'clock, and they were fifteen minutes late.

Example 3

Man: Most people don't realize that Jim's father is my older brother.

Example 4

Woman: Annie cut short her vacation when she heard that her was sick.

Example 5

Man: Jake is a doctor like his father and his father's father.

NOW YOU TRY

Choose the sentence that restates the sentence you hear.

1. Woman: The exam results won't be known until early October.

2. Man: He paid $3,000 for his new motor cycle; that's $400 more than it would have cost last year.

3. Woman: Rose lost 7 pounds on a diet, but her mother lost twice as much.

4. Man: Although I studied hard for the test, there were many questions I couldn't answer.

5. Woman: She bought a second–hand computer for $1,500. That's just half of what new one could cost.

NOW TURN OFF THE TAPE AND CHECK YOUR ANSWERS.

DAY 2: Listening Comprehension Part B

Example 1

Woman: Hello. Is this the Admissions Office? I'd like to talk to Barbara, please.

Man: I'm sorry. Barbara is out with the flu. She won't be in before Monday.

Why wasn't Barbara at work today?

Example 2

Woman: Richard, could you lend me a hand tomorrow? I need to clear the junk out of the garage and could use some help.

Man: Sure, I'd be happy to help, but I'm not free until after lunch. Is that okay?

What does the woman ask the man to do?

NOW YOU TRY

Choose the letter that best answers the question you will hear after each conversation.

1. Man: Why are you returning that scarf? It's pretty!

   Woman: Oh, I got it for my birthday, but I never wear scarves.

   Why is the woman returning the scarf?

2. Man: Nancy, I'll pick you up in an hour, if that's all right.

   Woman: That's fine. I'll see you at seven.

   What time is it now?

3. Man: Judy, I thought you were going to have the repairman come over to fix the washing machine today.

   Woman: I tried to call him all morning, but his phone seems to be out of order.

   Why didn't the repairman fix the washing machine?

4. Woman: I'm sorry, I can't cash your traveller's checks without some identification such as a driver's license.

   Man: Here's my passport–will this do?

   Why does the man need identification?

5. Woman: Hello, Mr. Holt. Is my prescription ready?

   Man: It's right here, Mrs. Grunder. Just follow the directions and take two capsules after every meal.

   Where does the man work?

6. Man: Say, why don't you and your husband come over for lunch next Sunday?

Woman: We'd love to, but we plan to visit my parents then. It's my father's birthday.

Where will the woman and her husband go for Sunday lunch?

7. Man: Your plane tickets to Paris are ready, Mrs. Hughes. You may come in and pick them up whenever it is convenient. You leave Dallas on the evening flight as requested.

Woman: Thank you, I'll come by this afternoon.

Where is the woman planning to go?

8. Man: Are you still planning to buy a new car?

Woman: Yes, but not until I get back from my summer vacation.

What will the woman do first?

9. Woman: Help yourself to more meat loaf and vegetables, Frank. There's plenty.

Man: Thanks, Ms. Dolan. The food is delicious, but I really couldn't eat another bite.

What will the man not do?

10. Man: There's an ad here for a part-time secretary. Working hours are flexible and the salary is negotiable.

Woman: What's the number? I'll call and find out if I can go for an interview.

What are the man and woman looking for?

Now turn off the tape and check your answers.

DAY 3: Listening Comprehension Part C

Example 1

Man: Tobacco was unknown to Europeans until Columbus reached America. Native Americans used tobacco in their religious ceremonies.They smoked it in pipes and chewed it. They also used snuff. Columbus returned to Europe with tobacco samples, but few people there used tobacco until 1580. In that year, Sir Walter Raleigh started a smoking fad in Europe. Raleigh was a very popular person in the court of Queen Elizabeth I. When he started smoking, many people copied him. Smoking soon spread to other European countries and to England's colonies in Africa and Asia.

1. What is the main idea of this passage?
2. Who introduced tobacco to the Europeans?
3. When did tobacco become popular in Europe?
4. Who made tobacco popular in Europe?

Example 2

Woman Suppose you run a race. During the exercise your heart beats faster . . . . What makes this happen? The answer is that extra carbon dioxide is produced by your muscles and this starts to build up in your bloodstream. The brain senses this is happening, and it sends nerve impulses to the heart making it beat faster. This is an automatic reflex: it happens without you having to think about it. The result of the heart beating faster is that more blood can be sent to the muscles.

5. What is the main idea of this passage?
6. What starts to build up in your bloodstream when you run?

7. What is the result of the heart beating faster?

Example 3

Man: I hear you're finally going to visit the Statue of Liberty.

Woman: Sure. It will be one of the highlights of my trip to New York. I'll send you a postcard.

Man: I guess you know the Statue was originally a gift from France in 1884, but do you know about the pedestal?

Woman: The pedestal? What's so special about that?

Man: Well, the statue was a gift, but Americans were asked to raise the money to pay for its base or pedestal by contributing to a special fund.

Woman: Now that I didn't know! When was the Statue finally completed?

Man: It was finally finished and dedicated in 1886. It still stands on its original site in New York Harbor.

8. What are these people talking about?

9. When was the Statue brought to the US?

10. Why did Americans contribute to a fund?

NOW YOU TRY

Choose the correct answers to the questions you will hear after the passage.

Passage 1

Man: When planning a fitness program, you should consider health precautions. It is good to begin planning your program with a complete medical checkup. Individuals who are very overweight or who have medical problems may need to start out with low intensity activities. If that is true in your case, exercise for longer periods of time at a slower pace. Walking briskly for 45 to 60 minutes is a good exercise. You will gain cardiorespiratory benefits even if your heartbeat does not reach your target range. Eventually, you will be able to do more intense exercise.

Low back pain is a common problem for many people. Some back problems and muscle and joint strains can be caused by improper exercise technique. Be sure to do the exercises as instructed. If you have a heart problem, weak back, knee problem, or any other condition that may limit your physical activity, discuss your problem with your doctor when planning an exercise program.

1. Who is probably giving this talk?

2. What should you do before starting your fitness program?

3. What is a good low-intensity activity for people who are overweight or have medical problems?

4. What may be the cause of some back problems?

Passage 2

Woman: Say, Frank, these tiny cheese triangles are delicious! Don't tell me you made them yourself.

Man: Sure I did! Taking that international cooking course was really worthwhile–I learned a lot.

Woman: Well, this pastry is delicious. How about giving me the recipe?

Man: Ah, that's called filo pastry. It's extremely popular in the Middle East. In the old days people would make their own filo at home from flour and water. It is really a time-consuming task because of the amount of rolling and stretching needed to make it thin enough. So I suggest you do what I do.

Woman: Which is?

Man: I buy it already prepared and keep it in the freezer until I need it! But when you use it, always keep the pastry covered with a damp cloth to prevent it from drying out.

5. What is the woman interested in knowing?

6. According to the man, where is this type of pastry popular?

7. How can you prevent the pastry from drying out?

Passage 3

Man: In many ways Madrid remains Europe's most underrated capital city, although its selection as the 1992 cultural capital of Europe has done much to change this image. The city has as many museums as London, plus an outdoor sculpture park, and a fabulous permanent collection of modern art at the Reina Sofia Center.

There's a program of events for the whole year, but May is a particularly good month in Madrid. The city's patron saint is celebrated with outdoor music and processions during the San Isidro festival which is held from May 12th through the 30th. The weather is also pleasant at this time of year–although it should be noted that the Metro, Madrid's efficient subway, does have air conditioning.

The best area for accommodation in Madrid is around the spectacular red and white 17th century Plaza Mayor Square, and away from the main highways. This is an area of small shops, squares, craftsmen, galleries, cinemas lively cafes and restaurants. You can still buy dinner here for 10 dollars per person, and it's customary not to eat until 10 or 11 P.M.

8. Why was the year 1992 important for Madrid?

9. When is the patron saint's festival held?

10. Which is the best area to look for somewhere to stay?

Now turn off the tape and check your answers.

DAY 10: PART 2 The Mini TOEFL Test

Section 1: Listening Comprehension

Part A: Choose the sentence that restates the sentence you hear.

1. Man: Bob couldn't figure out what the matter with Alison was.

2. Woman: Chuck asked his wife to pick up his suit from the cleaners.

3. Man: Dennis lent of $50 to each of his two sisters.

4. Woman: Isn't Celeste's dress for the prom absolutely gorgeous!

Part B: Choose the letter that best answers the question you will hear after each conversation.

5. Man Did you ask Richard if he'd like to come to the barbecue Thursday night?

   Woman: I've been dialing his number all day but keep getting a busy signal.

   Will Richard come to the barbecue?

6. Woman: Is this the accounts department? I'd like to speak to the manager.

   Man: If you'll just hold the line, I'll get Mr. Hartung.

   What does Mr. Hartung do?

7. Woman: Don't worry about the VCR. I'll see what's wrong with it when I get home from work tonight.

   Woman: I'd feel much happier if you'd just let me call the repairman.

   What does the woman want?

Part C: Choose the correct answers to the questions you will hear after the passage.

Woman: A woman's nutrition during pregnancy is very important to the health of her baby and herself. The baby is growing very fast and building tissues.To help her child grow well, the mother needs to supply all the baby's nutrients. The need for protein, calcium, phosphorus, magnesium and folic acid is especially great at this time. An undernourished mother will give birth to a smaller, less healthy baby. She may also harm herself. For example, if she gets too little calcium, the body will use its own calcium to supply the baby. This can weaken the mother's bones and teeth.

An adult woman who already eats a well-balanced diet will need to make only small changes to supply more of these nutrients. Calorie needs increase by 15 percent, or about 300 extra calories per day.

8. What can weaken the mother's bones and teeth?

9: How many extra calories will a pregnant woman on a well–balanced diet need?

10. An undernourished mother runs the risk of giving birth to which of the following?

Now turn off the tape and check your answers.

Acknowledgments

LISTENING PASSAGES (as transcribed under Tapescript)

DAY 3: EXAMPLE 1

Bud Getchell, Rusty Pippin and Jill Varnes, Perspectives on Health, (Lexington, Massachusetts: D.C. Heath and Company, 1992), p.344.

EXAMPLE 2: M.B.V. Roberts, Biology for Life, 2nd ed. (Walton-on-Thames, Surrey: Nelson, 1986), p.215.

PASSAGE 1: Bud Getchell, Rusty Pippin and Jill Varnes, Perspectives on Health, (Lexington, Massachusetts: D.C. Heath and Company, 1992), p.268.

PASSAGE 3: Susan Marling, "Europe Revisited," Good Housekeeping Magazine, April, 1992.

DAY 10: PART C

Bud Getchell, Rusty Pippin and Jill Varnes, Perspectives on Health, (Lexington, Massachusetts: D.C. Heath and Company, 1992), p.165.

READING PASSAGES

DAY 9 (PART 1)

PASSAGE 1: Janet R. Swinton and William J. Agopsowicz, Read and Respond (Los Angeles, California: Roxbury Publishing Company, 1987), pp.40-1.

PASSAGE 2: Bud Getchell, Rusty Pippin and Jill Varnes, Perspectives on Health, (Lexington, Massachusetts: D.C. Heath and Company, 1992), p.247.

PASSAGE 3: "Lead and Your Kids," from NEWSWEEK, February 17 (C)1992, Newsweek, Inc. All rights reserved. Reprinted by permission.

PASSAGE 4: "A Blood Test," from NEWSWEEK, April 20, (C)1992, Newsweek, Inc. All rights reserved. Reprinted by permission.

PASSAGE 5: "Return to Go and Collect 2,000 ECUs," from NEWSWEEK, April 20, (C)1992, Newsweek, Inc. All rights reserved. Reprinted by permission.

DAY 9 (PART 2)

PASSAGE 6: Schraer and Stoltze, Biology the Study of Life (Englewood Cliffs, N.J.: Prentice-Hall Inc., 1991), p.804.

PASSAGE 7: "Noriega: How the Feds Got Their Man," from NEWSWEEK, April 20, (C)1992, Newsweek, Inc. All rights reserved. Reprinted by permission.

PASSAGE 8: Charles F. Gritzner, World Geography (Lexington MA: DC Heath and Company, 1989), pp. 143-4.

PASSAGE 9: "Tapping the Secrets of Sleeping Bears," INTERNATIONAL HERALD TRIBUNE, April 23, 1992.

DAY 10 (SECTION 3)

"Losing Ground," from NEWSWEEK, April 6, (C)1992, Newsweek, Inc. All rights reserved. Reprinted by permission.

"Saving Gallons," from NEWSWEEK, February 24, (C)1992, Newsweek, Inc. All rights reserved. Reprinted by permission.